W9-BRC-017

I
HAVE HEARD
YOU CALLING
IN THE
NIGHT

OTHER BOOKS BY THOMAS HEALY

A Hurting Business
Rolling
It Might Have Been Jerusalem

I HAVE HEARD YOU CALLING IN THE NIGHT

★ * ★

THOMAS HEALY

HARCOURT, INC.

Orlando Austin New York San Diego Toronto London

Requests for permission to make copies of any part of the work should be
submitted online at www.harcourt.com/contact or mailed to the following
address: Permissions Department, Harcourt, Inc., 6277 Sea Harbor Drive,
Orlando, Florida 32887-6777.

www.HarcourtBooks.com

First published in Great Britain by Granta Books.

Library of Congress Cataloging-in-Publication Data
Healy, Thomas, 1944–
I have heard you calling in the night/Thomas Healy.—1st U.S. ed.
p.   cm.
1. Healy, Thomas, 1944– .   2. Dog owners—Scotland—Biography.
3. Alcoholics—Scotland—Biography.   4. Doberman pinscher—Scotland.
5. Human-animal relationships—Scotland.   I. Title.
SF422.82.H42H43   2006
636.73'6092—dc22   2006006363
ISBN-13: 978-0-15-101259-6   ISBN-10: 0-15-101259-8

Text set in Minion
Designed by Lauren Rille

Printed in the United States of America
First U.S. edition
K J I H G F E D C B A

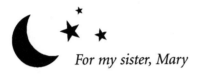

For my sister, Mary

I HAVE HEARD YOU CALLING IN THE NIGHT

* * ★

It seems now like a different me, the years I spent with
Martin, a Doberman dog, and before he came, another
me; and it is a new me now, once again, writing this. I
would have been dead long ago had I continued to live the
way I had before he came. I think someone would have
murdered me, given how I drank and the dives that I
drank in and that I was an aggressive, angry man. I had no
money and no friends. I didn't care, I couldn't have.

How this state of affairs had come to be I don't know,
for I had been a friendly if timorous boy and had managed
to dodge violence until I was twenty, when I had a run in
with a man named Bull Flannigan. By that time I was

working for the railway as a shunter in a yard in Spring-burn in Glasgow. The job was shifts and there was lots of overtime and I remember that I was able to save four pounds a week, which was a lot of money in 1964. You could buy eleven or twelve pints of beer for one pound then.

I had got into the habit of an occasional pint in a pub that was just under a bridge from the shunting yard. Springburn was a tough district, full of scarred and battered faces: teenage gangs and individual hard men. The man with the hardest reputation was Bull Flannigan. If you were in a pub and he was there, you looked the other way.

When I was working in the shunting yard I would have jumped if a girl had said boo. But I was a good enough shunter and worked all the overtime I could get, and I always had money. I was good for a loan, a couple of pounds to a fellow shunter until payday. I sometimes gave a loan inside the pub, which Bull Flannigan might have noticed, clocked up. Or someone might have told him. There are always people who want to keep on the right side of a fellow like Flannigan in Glasgow pubs.

Flannigan was in his thirties and had a close-cropped, too-big head. He was low and squat and wore a buttoned-up black crombie coat. Most of the time he was with two other men who also wore black crombie coats. But not that night.

I had been alone at the bar when, out of nowhere, he was standing next to me. I felt weak to fall by his very presence: a super hard man. I was told to buy him a whisky, and given a push on my chest so that I got the message.

The barman and some customers were looking on. The young railway man and Bull Flannigan: a small drama. I was as frightened as I had ever been, but at the same time I did not see why I should buy him a whisky. The easy way out would have been to have bought the whisky and got the hell away from Bull Flannigan. There was nobody who would have looked down on me had I done that, but I could not. Everything in me said no. This bullying hard man in his crombie coat. I told him to buy his own whisky.

A pause. I saw a first doubt in Flannigan's eyes. They were blue, for what that matters. I was taller than him, but he was thicker. They did not call him Bull for nothing. And an insistent bull, that I buy him a whisky. I was now seeing red. Flannigan made to push me again, and I punched him on the nose. Hard. I felt the bridge smash. He stumbled back, his nose ruined and his crombie coat bright with blood. Was this me, the trembling boy of a moment ago? I was a wild man now, hitting Flannigan. It was one-way punches. The first blow on his nose had done for him. And it had done for me, the boy I had been till then. When I left that pub I was a changed person. More a man? I thought so. But I wish now that I had never had that fight, for looking down the years, it did not change me for the better.

From the time of that first fight with Bull Flannigan until I was thirty-nine, I was seldom out of fights. My life was a blur of alcohol, flights of fancy, wild, drunken brawls. It is no use kidding here about my drinking habit. I was a paid-up alcoholic. I think the drinking game got out of hand when I was twenty-three, on holiday in Amsterdam. A tour round the bars, the red-light district. I did not feel right until I had had a few Amstel beers. I soon discovered a much stronger brew, stuff that came in small bottles, like half-pints. And no wonder: you could get drunk on four or five of them. This was the summer of 1967. The world was swinging. I was rolling, falling down. And I would go on falling for many years to come. No matter how much I drank, there was never enough, that was the way I was.

In 1983, with forty approaching, I thought to begin anew, to remove myself to London. I had no idea what I would do there, but the place appealed to me, as, over the years, it has appealed to a lot of lost and lonely men. I was assisted in this plan by the offer of a film deal on one of my short stories. I was a writer—not that I was doing much writing then. But in March of that year a man named Martin Harrington offered to buy the film rights to a story of mine. We had spoken on the telephone and agreed to a sum of money. Some hundreds. I thought it enough to get started in London. A couple of days later I got an early-morning train, a one-way ticket. I had no intention of returning to Glasgow.

I met Harrington in Euston Station. He had a bald head and a big black beard. We went for a drink, and, really, it was no big deal—I had won more money on the horses. Harrington struck me for a cagey guy and I can't say that I liked him. A mutual feeling, I am sure. But I got the money, a bunch of notes in a pub. I had a good drink in me, and I forget how I got rid of Harrington—or how he got rid of me. So far as I know the story was never filmed, or, if it was, it must have flopped. The next I remember I was in the West End, the bright lights.

My new life? It had no chance, there was another fate awaiting me.

I had expected a whale of a time in London, but that night I took a taxi back to Euston and a night train back to Glasgow. I'm not sure why. On the train I was in a queer, blue mood. I knew I had been this way too much, too often in my life. In the morning, rumpled and hungover, I walked from the Central Station to St Enoch Square, where I got a number 7 bus. It no longer runs, not from St Enoch.

I was staying in my mother's house. Only a mother would have put up with me, for I could swing to violence easily, on a wrong word. I drank morning and night and through the night, and in this dismal state I hated myself for what I was, what I had become, and I had unreal fears and I felt not a little lonely.

I would have won a sissy competition, the boy I used to be. In the Gorbals, when the Gorbals was the Gorbals. About the worst place in the whole damn world for a sissy to grow up in. I got teased mercilessly, because I much preferred to hop and skip and play with girls than rough and tumble with the boys, which did not please my father. He was an old-school type of man and, unlike my mother, who used to laugh at it, he did not think it funny that girls should come to our door asking for me to go out and play with them.

He told my mother that he could not understand it and that I must have taken after her side of the family. 'It beats me, him,' he said. I would doubt that my father was ever a sissy, but who can tell? Different boys and different men in different times. My first reading, after picture books, was *Billy Bunter,* and I used to badger him to send me to Bunter's school. It seemed such fun. There was no rough-housing. My father told me that he had no money, and one night, in bed—we slept together for a short time— he told me that he loved me and even if he had the money I would not be going to Bunter's school.

This was a bit of a let-down. I would have left him and Glasgow double quick to join up with Bunter and Bob Cherry and Harry Wharton and Ram Singh and all the other boys at Greyfriars. A jolly lot who did not want to fight. A paper chase was more their idea of fun, when they were not playing cricket. But it was not to be, not for me, and rather than in school with Bunter I was stuck in Glasgow.

My father was good company. He could be tremen-dously affectionate. Sometimes, nights in bed together, he would tell me stories, mostly about boxing, which was a big thing to him and would become a big thing to me.

We would sometimes wrestle and I would sometimes fall asleep in his arms, laughing in that bed. It is a lasting memory. In bed with him: how safe and secure I felt!

★ * ★

My father had his pet, a black tomcat named Darkie. He had acquired it as a kitten from a quarry, and it would follow him around the house and sit on his knee when he sat in his chair.

Darkie was an unusually large and loyal cat and he was more than fond of it. Him. I think my father thought that Darkie was more than just a common cat, and he was *his* cat, and the one time we fell out was because of Darkie. I saw another side to my father that night, after I had lost his cat. "You stupid boy." Those were his actual words. He was in a cloth cap and heavy, steel-shod work boots. "I'll need to go out and look for him."

"Why did you take his cat out for a walk?" my mother asked after he had gone. "You know how he feels about Darkie."

"It went for me," I said, and so it had. Our walk. I had tied a piece of string on Darkie, like he was a dog. "I had to let it go."

"I hope he finds it."

So did I. My father's face. His cat. It had been the closest he had ever come to hitting me. A stupid boy! I had seen no harm in trying to walk Darkie. He had gone not badly to begin. On the street. A few paces. It was summertime and there were lots of people and I let go of his leash, if that's the word, and away went Darkie. A wild thing. He would have sprung for my face and I did not care if I never saw him again.

But of course I did. A mew at our door, and then he was scratching at the wood of it. My mother opened the door and let him in. "I wonder where your daddy is?"

"I don't care where he is."

"But Darkie's back."

"I can see that Darkie's back."

"Do you not like Darkie anymore?"

I shook my head. "No," I said. "I don't trust Darkie anymore."

And that was that. Me and Darkie. We were forced to stay in the same house but from that day we ignored each other.

My father was dead and so was Darkie by the time I acquired a dog, a young cross-breed, that because of his golden color I had christened Goldie. Not that I was much better, braver, even then, though a protection thing was coming to be big in me; I would let no one harm Goldie. He came from the dog pound. But it was a brief affair, for the dog had been sick, I think with distemper, and inside of a week, he had to be put down. I was a might sad boy that day; I can remember it yet, my feeling inside when Goldie was no more.

It was my habit on drinking bouts to buy the *Glasgow Herald,* an old favourite. I had once written for it, and it is safe to say that booze had cost me a job on it. The job could have turned my life, but it was not to be. I had continued drinking and I was still drinking. Cans of super-lager.

It was April now and a hint of summer, and I hated April and the longer nights, the bright, bright summertime. Reading the *Herald* one day, my eyes fell on the livestock column, pups for sale. I do not know why I paused at an ad for Doberman pups, which were coloured black and tan and were six weeks old and of a good pedigree. I had not thought to obtain a pet. But when I saw that telephone number in the *Herald,* all of a sudden I remembered Goldie and I wanted a dog. The Doberman breed appealed to me, so I telephoned the number. The man who answered told me to come round any time and see the pups, and as he was not too far away I told him that I would be round within the hour. He was tinkering with a motorbike when I arrived. Straight off I did not like the look of him. He was a beefy sort with a scar on his face. You get lots of guys like him in Glasgow.

'Are you the guy who telephoned?'

I said I was. I was half drunk and in need of a wash and a clean shirt. He had to think that he had found a clown, a drunken fool. He led me inside a tenement and up some stairs to a council flat. It was the sort of place that you would have thought twice about going if it was night and you were sober.

There were about six pups locked inside an airless room, on a filthy carpet. The rancid room was in need of fumigation. I had expected a more hygienic setting, and I disliked the fat man even more. I think about the only thing that he had done was feed the pups, who, despite the filth of their confine, appeared to be bright and full of fun, one tumbling over the other.

I asked where the mother was.

'She's in the other room.'

'I'd like to see her.'

'You must be kidding.'

'I'm not kidding.'

'She'd take off your arm if she knew why you were here.'

'Why, are you going to tell her?'

He hemmed and hawed. I almost laughed. Wherever he had got the litter, he did not have the mother. I had got down on my haunches and was quite taken by one particularly bold, aggressive pup. This small creature had fixed itself on to the back of my hand. It had sharp, cat-like claws and would not let go. Nor budge an inch. A show of affection? I thought so, and if it wanted me I wanted it and I decided to buy the pup.

The asking price was 150 pounds. There was no way I was paying that, not to him. I was standing again, with the pup on the back of my hand. I offered fifty pounds for it. He shook his head, that it was not enough. I told him he could take it or leave it for I was taking the pup, one way or the other. Afterwards people would think that I had got Martin for nothing, but he cost me fifty pounds.

This was all on a whim, the whole thing. I told the fat guy to phone a taxi for me and my new buddy on the back of my hand. He was all big black eyes and, for all I knew, he could have been a she. It took me weeks to determine its sex, to look.

I was drunk for all of the first week of our new guest's stay. The wee dog—that is what my mother called him— had slept against my chest when I sat drinking, or sleeping, in my chair. Or so my mother told me when I sobered up. She had cleaned up after him and had fed him tins of puppy food. She had no idea how he had come to be in our house, and had felt sorry for him. I think my mother thought I would get rid of him when I sobered up.

It would be touch and go for a good three weeks if he stayed or if he went. I had come by him when I was drunk and without a thought to his wants and needs. That I would need to buy a collar for him, for one thing. As it turned out, my mother bought him his first collar, a light tartan affair more suited to a poodle than a Doberman. He had to have been about three months old by then, when he got his collar.

How he had managed to stay I do not know. There had been times when I could have seen him far enough. The house-training. It had crossed my mind to return him to the fat guy, but I just could not do it. And, one week to two, a month, the longer he was with me, and he was with me all the time, the more I felt that he was my responsibility.

My sister Mary hit on a name for him. 'Tulip.'

'I don't like Tulip.'

'He came in April.'

'What's that got to do with Tulip?'

'They grow tulips in Holland in April,' she said.

They did? But I would not name my pup Tulip. It was not him, not even then. 'You can't have a boy dog with a name like Tulip.'

'Martin, then,' she said. 'Call him Martin.'

It sounded not too bad to me, and a whole lot better than her first choice, Tulip.

'If it hadn't been for that guy Martin Harrington you would never have had him.'

So Martin it was, and I have never heard of another dog called Martin.

On our first few walks I had Martin on a washline rope, and this had to appear odd, as though I had stolen him or something. I had a couple of offers to sell him, and for more money than the 150 pounds that the fat guy had been looking for. But there was never any question, not once I had become accustomed to him, that I would sell Martin.

His tail was docked and, for a while, I thought he had been born that way, with a short, stumped tail. I knew so much about dogs, the Doberman breed.

But I was beginning to know Martin. He was a prideful pup and given to sulk, to stay away from me for hours if I had scolded him.

My mother used to say, Martin sitting alone in a corner, 'The wee dog's fell out with Thomas.'

This went on for a time, that Martin could fall out with me, like take the humph and who did I think I was?

I was none too sure. And what was I doing with him? But we went together, somehow. Martin had learned my name before he knew his own. In the coming years there would be a mix-up over this, our names: I was sometimes Martin and he was sometimes Thomas.

For the first few weeks Martin slept at the bottom of my bed. We would get up about ten. After a coffee I would take him out while my mother was cooking the breakfast. I ate fried eggs and sausages, which I would carry through to the living room. We had a glass-topped table and Martin would sit watching me, his mouth dripping. I used to give him the white of an egg. One morning I went to answer the telephone and while I was gone he ate the lot, my breakfast. I looked at him, he looked at me. What to do? I pretended to have noticed nothing and sat down to eat.

'What's this?' I looked at the plate and then at Martin. 'Who has stolen my food?' I scratched my head as though astonished. 'Did you see anybody?'

Martin's eyes were big and round at my strange behaviour. He had expected an instant scolding; I should have been angry with him. It would have been more like the thing.

'We have a thief in the house.' I tapped my fork against the plate and showed my teeth and shook my fist. 'Come, we will catch him, Martin.' I was up off of the seat and through to the bedroom, where I looked behind the curtains and under the bed. 'Where can he be?'

Martin's head was cocked, he had a quizzical look. Had I gone off my head? I think, if he could speak, he would have owned up then that he ate my breakfast.

My mother made a new one. She had got into the act. 'Who do you think it could have been?'

'I asked Martin if he saw anybody.'

'He couldn't have,' my mother said. 'Martin wouldn't let anybody eat your breakfast.'

'Then it will just need to remain a mystery, whoever ate my breakfast.'

'We'll keep an eye open tomorrow morning.'

'You bet,' I said, and I looked at Martin, who looked bemused at all of this. 'We'll keep an eye open tomorrow morning.'

The next day I put my breakfast on the glass-topped table and told Martin, who was about four months old by now, to guard it while I looked out the window.

I had my back to him, but only for a moment. It was enough for Martin to steal one of my two fried eggs. I looked first at the plate and then at him. He looked at me with big guiltless eyes. 'Good boy,' I said, and when I had finished my breakfast I gave him the white of the remaining egg.

This would go on for years. It became a rite that at breakfast time I would turn away and Martin would steal an egg.

We lived in the ground-floor flat in a tenement in a housing scheme and had our own front garden. The garden was helpful when I house-trained Martin. It had taken less than a week. He had, at this stage, when the egg business had first begun, yet to bark and I had begun to think that he might be barkless.

'Woof. Woof,' I encouraged him, and I cupped my hand behind my ear. 'Woof. Woof.'

But still nothing, or only the usual quizzical look I got from him when I acted daft.

⋆ * ★

I think I must have been, a little. Daft. For when Martin did begin to bark, like find his voice, there would be no stopping him, "Woof. Woof." At the slightest little noise, "Woof. Woof." It was only after I had attended the Doberman Club that I learned to quieten him down.

"*Silence,* Martin," I would say, and press my finger to my lips, "we don't want to wake the dead, do we?"

This usually worked, if, for a time, him watching me, me watching him, we had to look like thieves.

⋆ * ★

Some teenage gangs hung around near to where we lived, and Martin used to growl at them. They called me Batman and he was Robin, and the name stuck. We were not a pair to mess with and the gangs avoided us and we avoided them. Or I did. Martin was for attacking them. We were neither of us popular. Martin was hardly a dog to pat. He disliked strangers. I suppose that I encouraged it, for I disliked strangers too.

The teenage gangs thought of themselves as wide boys and were well aware that I sometimes took too much to drink. One evening early that summer, I was much the worse for drink and collapsed in the field behind the house. This was the field where I took Martin every morning before breakfast. It was attached to a school and there was a football pitch, but we kept to the waste ground to the side. This was fenced off from the houses and it was pretty private and, on summer nights, it was a favoured haunt for the gang boys and their girls.

Some of the girls were as bad as the boys and it was their duty to hide the weapons, knives and open razors in their handbags until the need arose to use them. This was hardly new. I could remember the same practice when I was in my teens in the tenement Gorbals. When a fight did happen, and it could happen very suddenly, the girls, all shrieks and screams, would urge on the boys to greater deeds of derring-do. I had seen a couple of gang fights when I was in this field with Martin. But I had been sober then.

I was far from sober on this particular summer's evening. I staggered to collapse, pass out. A stricken Batman. Robin, though, was most alert, and when I came to he had his head on my belly and I had a bag of booze beside me on the ground. The gang boys and girls had let us be because they were scared of Robin. I was supposed to be in charge of him, but it had been the other way round that night.

★ * ★

Later that summer Martin took ill. When I brought him to the vet I was told that he had been poisoned. Until then I had let him out into the garden alone, and as it was the only place where he had been alone, it was the only place where he could have been poisoned.

Somebody trying to get back at me? I could think of a few who might want to, due to my past behaviour. I had suspicions of about ten persons, any one of whom could have been the poisoner. After he recovered I never let Martin out into the garden alone again.

It had been a close thing, for a time, if he would recover. The vet thought fifty-fifty. A listless Martin. He would neither eat nor drink. I was given a nutrient that I had to feed him from a dummy teat. By then Martin had shifted out from my bed to a couch that was beside the bed. I had thought it only right that we had separate sleeping quarters. We were still close enough, him on his couch and me in my bed, that Martin did not feel alone. Or, perhaps more to the truth, that neither of us felt alone. And I did not want to be alone again, without him. I think it was then, when Martin was ill, a poorly bit of fur and bone that I nursed all night with the dummy teat, that our bond was formed.

Before Martin's illness, I could not have believed that I would sit with him all through the night and will him to get better. Which I did, and he did. On the third or fourth night I saw the light come back into Martin's eyes. He licked my hand. A dry tongue. I got him water. When he began to lap the water I knew that we had won.

I never found out who had poisoned Martin, and as I was a much different man then than I am today, that was just as well.

Within days of his drink of water Martin was back to his bouncing self, and he had me and I had him.

When Martin arrived my mother was seventy-three. She had white hair and all of that but I did not think of her as old or elderly or that she was even ageing. She had always been there and had always been much the same to me. She had always worked and she was still working. She had a job as a cleaner in a bowling club. It was heavy work for a woman of her age, but I can't remember a single day when my mother was sick, laid up. In any case I did not give a thought to it. What money she earned she tried to save to go on holiday with a group of women she had known for years. They had been to Florida and Italy, the Channel Islands. Unlike me, she was a social person and well liked. There was nobody ever had a bad word to say about my mother. Wee Mrs Healy, she was barely five foot tall but had a big heart. She had survived my father's death and the death of a baby daughter. Her only two brothers had died on her, each one under fifty. You could safely say she had been through the mill and had known her share of sorrow. She had me for a son, after all. Over the years I must have been a tremendous worry to her. And now, as all of a sudden, I had a pal and my mother did not know what to make of him. Not at first. She had been told that he was a Doberman and that Dobermans were fierce guard dogs. Whoever had told her this had also said that you could never trust a Doberman.

'Are you keeping him, Thomas?'

'That's up to you. I can't keep him if you don't want him in the house.'

'I didn't say that I didn't want him in the house.'

This was after I had just sobered up and before I was fond of Martin. Before she was fond of Martin.

'If you're frightened of him.'

'I'm not frightened of him now,' she said. 'But it might be different when he grows up.'

'I don't think it will be different.'

And neither it was. Martin, a dog you could not trust? We trusted him with our lives, my mother and sister and me. But he was a one-man dog and at his happiest with me.

Mary took to Martin straight off. There was no problem with her about his staying. But it was me who had to look after him, she made that clear. 'He's your dog, not mine.'

It would soon become more than obvious to everyone whose dog Martin was. A new side to my nature? It had been a big surprise to a lot of people to see me with a pup. They had not thought that I was a doggy sort of man. Well, neither had I, but we all surprise ourselves sometimes. I suspect they thought it was a fad and that Martin would soon go, that I would kick him out in a drunken rage. They had to be disappointed when, week after week, he was still there. Far from a kick, it is my proud boast that I never laid a hand on Martin. He was never cowed or frightened of me. I encouraged his high spirits, a natural boldness. It was the way he was and why I chose him—or, as my mother often said, he chose me—when he had climbed up on to my hand and would not let go.

★ * ★

That autumn my mother and Mary went on holiday. It was just me and Martin in the house. Mary had warned me not to drink because of Martin.

'You're all he's got.'

'I know I'm all he's got.'

'You know what happens when you drink.'

'I won't drink.'

'You could lose Martin if you do.'

'I won't lose Martin.'

And I didn't, and I did not drink either. I read books and tried to write and took my pal on long, long walks. This was late September. You could feel the winter creeping in. A first frost. I felt to have come a long way since April. I was with my dog and I was sober.

I had been sober for most of that summer. An occasional slip now and then, but nothing compared to my former drinking. I was learning new things about myself. That I was as big a sucker for affection, even from a dog, as any man who ever lived. Martin brought out the boy in me. The surprise was that, in my basic nature, I had hardly changed at all. In many ways I was ten years old in the body of a man. I was not hard at all.

Mary could not believe the change in Martin when she returned from holiday.

'Are you sure that is the same dog?'

'No, I went out and bought another one.'

'He looks formidable.'

'In two weeks?'

'I'm telling you.'

'I didn't notice any change in him.'

'That's because you've been with him every day.'

'He's still the same Martin.'

But she was right, he was becoming big. A sudden sprout. High and rangy, a gangly look. But he was beginning to form and he had heavy bones and big paws, a promise of great power.

'You didn't drink.'

'Not a drop.'

'Did you miss it?'

'I didn't even think about it.'

'Then you don't need to drink, do you?'

No, I didn't. But a couple of weeks later I did drink and ended up in jail. In a police station in the Gorbals. I had been drinking all day and that night I got into a fight, a bad one. I emerged unscathed but the chances were that I would be remanded to prison for some time.

Inside the van on the way to court I could only think of Martin and what would become of him if I was sent to prison.

In court I was charged with assault. I pleaded not guilty. There were a couple of other guys involved and they pleaded not guilty too. We were all released to appear at a later date. To this day I still don't know why we were not sent to prison.

When I got home Martin almost knocked me down, so eager was his welcome.

The charge against me was later dropped because of insufficient evidence. But I wished I had not been in jail, even for a night. I felt more guilty about abandoning Martin than what they had charged me with. When I should have been looking out for both of us I had been chancing time in prison. I vowed never again for a similar predicament, and I have kept my vow and have had no trouble with the police since that autumn night in 1983.

★ * ★

My daddy died when he was forty-six. I was thirteen. We had slept together on his last night and there had been nothing wrong with him, not then. He had a drink in him and I could smell the beer and I was to play football in the morning. I was playing football morning, noon and night then. It was a move away from my former self: I had lost interest in girly games. Football was the game for me and all the boys played football. On the street, and games of headers in the closes. I had progressed to be captain of the school side and this had earned me respect on the street and at school. I was a boy of note.

This pleased my father, who encouraged it: at last he had a normal son. We spoke about football in bed that night. I slept in blue pyjamas and him in his underpants. He was hard and lean with a hairy chest, and he had big rough hands and was heavy at the shoulders. Which was not surprising, the work he did. My father was a lugger in a quarry. He had to break huge stones with a ten-pound hammer. It was a hard way to make a living, and he advised me to get a trade, to become a joiner or bricklayer or such.

A tradesman was looked up to where I grew up, and it was a big thing if you got a trade when you left school. I didn't, couldn't. I wanted to become a motor mechanic, but I had no one to get me in. In those days you needed someone to get you in, to start an apprenticeship. Had my father lived, who knows? I had often thought I could have become a footballer and played for Glasgow Celtic.

My father was supposed to take me to watch Celtic on the following day of his last night, which was a Friday. He was dead before the Saturday kick-off. A heart attack on a bus on his way to work in the quarry. He was carried off the bus and died on the open road.

This was November 1957. A long time ago, but I still miss him. We had become great pals and he was the only hero I ever had. An upright man and a man of God. He loved his faith, the Catholic Church, and I have been told that he died in prayer. I have often thought that he could and should have been a priest.

I missed my father badly. The more I began to know the world and other men, the more I began to appreciate the father I had had.

My father's death brought changes. I was able to stay out much later, and if I did not join in a gang it was just sheer luck or, more likely, because I did not want to fight. The gang boys accepted this and I was pals with lots of boys in different gangs. This was when I turned fourteen and had a first interest in the local girls, other than being just friends. An all-boys boarding school had no appeal when I was fourteen. I was out prowling the streets, looking for girls. Standing at the corners. A lot of the streets were still gas-lit, and late at night you could hear the gas hiss in the mantles. The yellow-lighted house windows. Horsing around with the girls, dummy fighting. It was the easy way to steal a feel, to make some contact, and the girls were not complaining. It was all good fun, this first experimenting.

I was still fourteen when I went to a local cinema, the Paragon in Cumberland Street, where, in the newsreel—they used to show two films and have a newsreel in between in those days—I saw young people in a kibbutz in Israel. They were turning the desert green, into a garden, according to the newsreader. Such an abundance of happy, young people, both boys and girls—I thought it was the place for me. But how to go about getting there, to join in and help to make the desert green?

There were Jewish people in the Gorbals. It was where Glasgow's Jewish community had first settled when they came over from Eastern Europe. I went to see a rabbi and asked him about going to Israel.

'How do you know to ask about the kibbutz?'

'I saw it at the pictures. It was on in a newsreel. They are turning the desert into a garden.'

'And now you want to go and help them, to make this garden greener? Is that the reason you are here?'

'It is. I want to go to Israel and work in a kibbutz.'

'Have you told your mother what you want to do?'

'No. Not yet. I thought to write to her from Israel.'

'You did?'

'I did.'

'Israel is not next door, you know.'

'I didn't think it was.'

'What if you never got home again?'

'I might never *want* to get home again.'

'No, you might not,' the rabbi said, 'but I am sure that your mother would want to see you again.'

'She could come to Israel.'

'I didn't think of that.'

'I could send for her, after I have found my feet.'

The rabbi sat in an easy chair beside a coal fire, and I was sitting in another chair across from him. A tall, rather sad-faced man. We were not long after the war, from Hitler's ovens, in 1958. I would think the Jewish people were still uncertain about what might happen to them, at that time and after such atrocities. Six million dead. Was he humouring me? Was there a smile in his beard? I had appeared at his door out of nowhere, wanting to go to Israel.

'All this because of a newsreel,' he said.

'You want to have seen it. They sing at work and sleep in tents and pick lemons off of trees.'

'I think that it is oranges that they pick.'

'Will you help me get to Israel?'

The rabbi scratched his beard. He was dressed in a fisherman's jersey and had black, shiny shoes. I remember his shoes because, when he crossed his legs, I had noticed a hole in the sole of one of them. You would never catch a priest like that, with a hole in the sole of his shoe.

'I can't,' he said. 'You are too young.'

'I'm sixteen.'

'No you're not.'

'Fifteen.'

'Try again.'

'Nobody would miss me.'

'What about your mother?'

'I told you, I could write to her from Israel.'

The rabbi's wife—I had thought she was his house-keeper—was somewhere in the house and, at that, she could contain herself no longer, that I was a cruel and inconsiderate boy and that she had never heard the like of it, what I had proposed to do. 'You should hang your head in shame,' she said.

'Can I ask your name?' the rabbi asked me.

'It's Thomas.'

'My wife is Edith.'

Edith was a round, short, stubby woman. 'I have listened to it all,' she said. Then, looking to her husband, 'Did someone send you here?'

'No, nobody sent me here. Why should they? I haven't told anyone that I want to go to Israel.'

'Did you think my husband would send you there?'

'I didn't know.' What was this about? I was beginning to worry that Edith, if I disclosed my full name, would shop me to my mother. 'I saw a newsreel, that is all.'

'You then thought to involve my husband in your wicked plan?'

'I thought to ask for his advice on how best to get to Israel.'

'He doesn't know.'

'There is no harm done,' the rabbi told his wife. 'Thomas is just looking for adventure.'

'He should be in his bed at home.'

It was about eight or nine o'clock at night.

'I must see this newsreel,' the rabbi said.

'It's still on in the Paragon, if you want to go and see it.'

'You are still a schoolboy,' Edith said. 'You see a newsreel and after it you want to go to Israel.'

I looked at the rabbi. He was near to laughter now. 'Have you run away before?' he asked.

'For all we know he could be on the run right now,' Edith said.

'I'm not,' I said. 'This is the first time that I've thought to run away.'

'I pity your mother.'

I pitied the rabbi—the hole in his shoe and married to *her*.

'I've changed my mind about running away.'

'We should take you to the police,' Edith said, 'and make sure that you don't run away.'

'I don't think that there is any need for that,' her husband said.

'There *isn't*,' I said.

'What school do you attend?' Edith asked.

'I'm not telling you.' I was beginning to think to make a run for it, right out of the door. 'I don't want to get into trouble.'

'You could be getting *us* into trouble, did you not think of that?'

I was bamboozled, for I could not see how I could be getting *them* into trouble.

'If you did run away and something bad happened, then the police would begin to track your movements.'

'There's nobody would know that I was here.'

'*We* would know, and we would need to tell them.'

'But he won't run away, will you, Thomas?'

'I won't,' I said, and neither I would, or only out of the rabbi's house. 'I have told you, I have changed my mind.'

'You see my point, don't you, Lionel?' Edith asked the rabbi. 'I would be much happier if we knew his name at least.'

'He could give us a false name.' Lionel was touching his beard again. 'But we know how he looks, *if* he runs away.'

'I won't.'

'Let's hope you don't.'

Lionel walked me to the door. For some reason I was very aware of the hole in the shoe.

'Edith is excitable, but she means the best,' he told me.

'I thought that she was going to call the cops.'

The door led out of the house into a cobbled, gas-lit alley.

'They would have laughed at her if she had,' Lionel said.

'But they would have taken me home and told my mother.'

'What about your father?'

'He is dead.'

'When did he die?'

'About a year ago.'

'Do you still miss him?' Lionel was walking with me in the alley, going towards the street. 'I know that I missed my father when he died.'

'I try not to think about him.'

'What caused his death?'

'A heart attack. They called it a coronary thrombosis. It's hard for me to think he'll never come home again.'

'Did you think you could have forgotten all about him if you had got to Israel?'

'I could never forget *all* about him.'

'I'm glad you know that,' Lionel said, 'for there are some things, people, we can never forget, no matter how long we live or where we might go. You should try to remember that, Thomas.'

The alley we walked along had one rough-brick wall and the other wall was the synagogue.

'Do you say mass in there?' I asked.

'No, Jews don't have mass. I take it you are a Catholic, Thomas?'

'I am, but I would have become a Jew if it would have gotten me to Israel.'

'Just like that?'

'I mean, I could have become a Catholic again if I

didn't like being Jewish.' We had come out of the alley on to the street. 'But I might have liked being Jewish.'

'You are a most unusual young man.' I was pleased to have been called a young man. 'I shall think about you.'

The street looked wide and flat and it was sheened with rain. Lionel offered me a half-crown coin. 'Don't tell Edith, for she would tear her hair out.'

I did not doubt that. But I did not want his half-a-crown, I think because of the hole in his shoe.

'Can't you just say a prayer for me?'

'I shall pray for you anyhow,' Lionel said.

'I don't think you have much money.'

'A half-crown is not the end of the world.'

'I thought all Jews were rich.'

'Not this one, but I can afford half-a-crown.' It was quite a lift to me, a half-crown. I could go to the movies four, maybe five times. 'I had better get back, or Edith will think we have run away together.'

I laughed. 'So long!' I began to run down the street, the half-crown in my pocket.

I was restless to see the world, to get out of Glasgow, and about six weeks later teamed up with another boy and we ran away to London. He was a classmate at school, was Joseph McGuigan, a large, heavy boy with a roly-poly, beefy look. He stayed with his grandmother in a street not far from mine. We had a loose contact until, one day in the playground, I learned that he had once run away before and ended up in Blackpool. He was an adventurous one, I will say that about McGuigan, and he was all for it when I suggested we should run away together.

In the school playground, McGuigan had often spoken about going to sea and suggested I should join him. 'They would never find us then!' This time, though, he thought that we should go to London. He had relatives there who, so he said, would put us up and ask no questions. When I asked McGuigan how he knew they would ask no questions, he said that they were Irish tinkers, as if that explained it all. I did not think to ask how he knew where they would be, if they were tinkers. It was that crazy, the whole thing: McGuigan and me and running away! We stole aboard a night train bound for London.

I can't say I had given much thought in regard to my mother and sister, the anxiety that they would suffer when, about two in the morning, they would be looking for me and I was on the London train.

McGuigan had an eye for a chance and on the train he managed to steal a wallet. Until then we had no money and were travelling for free. There was a lot of moving about on that train, avoiding ticket collectors. We had to have been in and out of about ten compartments before McGuigan stole the wallet. Somewhere in the Midlands? We were way past Carlisle anyhow; I remember that the train changed engines—they were the old steam ones—when we were at Carlisle. That and new men checking for tickets. They were as easy to dodge as the first ones had been. Inside a toilet McGuigan emptied out the wallet. Some sixty pounds in ten-pound notes! It was the first real money I had seen. Half to him and half to me. I put my share in my shoe. The empty wallet was then thrown out of the window.

We must have been too tired to care about the ticket collectors, for soon after that we found an empty compartment and went to sleep. The next I knew, McGuigan was pushing me awake and the train was in Euston Station, London. 'We've made it,' he said. 'We're here!'

We were both hungry, almost starving. It had been early the previous evening since we had eaten. There were two more ticket collectors at the end of the platform, but we were beginning to be good at this and swerved them easily. We were soon out on to the concourse. I was surprised by all the people. Outside of a football match, I had never seen so many people in one place at one time. The gents with their brollies and bowler hats. There was a feeling of indifference, such a crowd. We were not paid the slightest heed. Here and there you could spy a policeman, and I was impatient to leave the station. But McGuigan insisted that we eat first. 'There's nobody looking for us,' he said. 'There's nothing to worry about.'

I was beginning to like McGuigan. He had an air of dare, that anything might happen. This belied the way he looked, all wobbling fat, as a youthful Oliver Hardy. He led the way inside the restaurant and we ordered up two English breakfasts. Fried eggs and beans and sausages. A pot of tea. I paid for the treat with a ten-pound note, looking at McGuigan. I think we had both prepared to run, if they did not accept the money. The ten-pound note looked so big and seemed too much to me; but the waiter barely glanced at it before giving me my change. Which seemed more like *real* money, one-pound notes and silver coins, copper pennies and a threepenny bit. I was richer than I had ever been and we had only just set out.

McGuigan suggested and I agreed that we should spend the day exploring. Piccadilly and Leicester Square and Madame Tussaud's waxworks. Later on we could set about tracking down his relatives, who, from the last he had heard, were in a London district named Cricklewood.

But just as I was beginning to look forward to our day's exploring, McGuigan was arrested for shoplifting. He had gone into a shop inside the station to steal some chocolate and not made it out of it, on to the London streets. It was a dreadful blow for my chubby pal and me. The last I saw of him, he was between two cops, being escorted from the station.

I almost went home. The whole deal had suddenly turned sour, the caught McGuigan. I had no idea what to do or where to go in London. Standing in the station, I was dressed in a zip-up jerkin and denim jeans. A man aged about thirty stepped right in front of me and I was invited for a coffee. Young as I was, I sensed something queer in this one. Coffee with a stranger? God knows how long he had been watching me. Perhaps since McGuigan had been arrested. I would not be at all surprised, given my age and where I was.

I told him no, but he persisted, now gripping the sleeve of my jerkin.

'You could be doing yourself a favour.'

'I don't want to do myself a favour.'

I snatched my arm away from him. He was wearing a long black coat and had a thin, white face. A foxy look. There were lots of people passing by, but no one gave a look to that man and me.

'I could make it worth your while,' he said.

'How do you mean, make it worth my while?'

'Come with me for a coffee and I'll explain.'

'Tell me *now*.'

'Do you have hairy balls?'

I made to walk away from him, but he was gripping my sleeve once more.

'Let me go!'

'Take it easy.'

I was frightened, but angry, and I almost flung my first punch then, there in Euston Station. This was the first I had been propositioned and I found it hard to credit.

'What are you doing in London?' he asked. He had let go of my sleeve and was standing back, a good foot away from me. 'Have you run away?'

'What's that to you?'

'I know other boys who have run away.'

'Where are they?'

'Here and there. I try to help them, if I can.'

I began to walk away from him, wishing McGuigan was with me. There would have been no problem with such a man if McGuigan had still been there. It is a huge remove from two to one, if you are fourteen and alone in London. But soon I left the man behind and, after looking round for him a couple of times, he was gone.

I don't know where I went that day, but I certainly walked for miles. I remember a blister on my foot and that I was hobbling somewhat because of it, when I stopped at a café for hot pies and beans and a cup of Bovril.

A couple of young teddy boys—they wore long drape jackets and suede shoes—sat down beside me.

'Where have you come from?' one of them asked.

'Glasgow. Can you tell me where I am?'

'You're in the East End. Near Bow Bells. Where did you think you was?'

'I didn't know.'

'Well, you know now.' The teddy boys were about eighteen or nineteen. 'Have you got a place to stay?' one asked.

'No, I don't have any place to stay. I only arrived in London this morning.'

'Where is your luggage?'

'I don't have luggage.'

'Are you on the trot?'

'The *trot*?'

'Is the law after you?'

'I think so.' I was almost sure McGuigan would have told the cops that I'd been with him. 'Do you know of a place where I can stay?'

They told me no, naturally, but that I should go to King's Cross. 'There's a lot of Scottish people there.'

A while later I was on a street in King's Cross speaking to a prostitute. Her name was Lily and she came from Glasgow.

'What are you going to do now?' she asked.

'I was hoping that you might help me.'

'I could give you a couple of pounds.'

'I'm looking for a place to sleep.'

'Are you asking me to put you up?'

'I don't have anybody else to ask to put me up.'

Lily had long dark hair and she was quite attractive in a gaudy way. This brassy place was full of cars and pubs and prostitutes and it was not yet eight o'clock.

'I would sleep on the floor.'

Lily wore a light white coat and a high, tight skirt and high-heeled shoes. I thought her to have been a fair age, but she was only twenty.

'I can't do anything *now*,' she said, 'but if you meet me here at ten o'clock we'll try to work something out.'

There were plenty of cafés and I ate more pies and beans and drank more Bovril, waiting. My new friend had work to do, but it was good at least I had a friend, someone to meet. King's Cross looked to be one tough place, as alive as a fuelled-up carnival. The prostitutes attracted men of every nationality, and there were some rough-looking customers. I wondered about McGuigan. Could he be on a train to Glasgow? The café was a dingy, white-lighted place. I sat well to the back, away from the window. The proprietor was a dark-skinned man who spoke in broken English. Other than Lily, I had spoken to no one. I was without a watch but the café had a round electric clock and I was able to time when to go, to meet again with Lily.

I met Lily where I had left her, near a red pillar box. She had been waiting for me.

'I wondered if you would still be here.'

'Where else could I go?'

'You could have been picked up. There's a lot of plain-clothed dicks in this place.'

'I was in a café.'

King's Cross was not so busy now, sex-wise; just a few last loitering prostitutes. But there were a lot of drunken revellers.

'I had pies and beans.'

'Then at least I won't need to feed you.'

'No, I'm full up.' I was a tall boy, touching six foot, and I towered over Lily, who was small, maybe five foot. 'Have you found me a place to stay?'

'You can stay with me, but only for tonight. What is your name anyhow?'

'Tam.'

'I'm Lily.'

'I know.'

'How do you know?'

'I heard someone call you Lily.' I was walking with her. I remember the hit of her heels against the ground, the pavements of King's Cross. 'Have you been doing this for long?'

'Do you mean have I been on the game for long? Since I first came to London. I was only sixteen and it was the easiest thing for me to do.'

'Do you make a lot of money?'

'Are you always as nosy?'

'I'm only curious.'

'I get by.' Lily was leading me down a lane where some couples were having sex together, almost in the open. 'A lot of the girls bring their punters here.'

I could not stop from watching them, white arses in the night.

'This is a different world,' I said.

'Have you never been to Blytheswood Square in Glasgow? I used to work there; it's much the same as this place.'

'Where did you *stay* in Glasgow?'

'I was brought up in the Gallowgate, near to the Barras.'

'I've been to the Barras.'

At the end of the lane we turned into a narrow, almost sunken street. Lily was a brisk walker and with my blistered foot I had trouble keeping up with her.

'It's not far now,' she told me.

'I've been walking all day.'

'I can see that, you're limping.' Lily took my hand. 'Are you still at school?'

I thought to lie and say no, but she had been kind to me and I told the truth, that I was still at school. 'But I hate it.'

'What school do you go to?'

'St Bonaventure's, it's in the Oatlands, but a lot of the boys from the Gorbals go there.'

'I've heard of it,' Lily said. 'I went to St Margaret's.'

'Then you're a Catholic?'

'I am, but it's a long time since I've been to chapel.' Lily laughed. 'Imagine me going into a confessional.'

'The priest can't tell on you,' I said, 'no matter what you've done.'

'I know that, but why should I tell a priest?'

'You might feel better afterwards.'

'Do *you* go to chapel?'

'No, not now, but I used to go when I was younger.' It was really nice, holding Lily's hand. 'I was thinking of becoming a Jew,' I said.

'Why would you want to do that?'

'I'd like to go to Israel, to a kibbutz. McGuigan, the boy I was with, wanted to go to sea and I would have gone with him if I could have got to Israel.'

'I've never heard of anything like this before. How did you find out about a kibbutz in Israel?'

'At the pictures. It was on a newsreel. In the Paragon in Cumberland Street.'

'I've heard of Cumberland Street, the Cumbie gang. Are you in it, Tam?'

'No, I don't like fighting. But there was a man today I wanted to punch. I met him in Euston Station after McGuigan had been arrested.'

'Did he ask to feel your arse or what, this man?'

'He asked if I had hairy balls.'

'Have you?'

'I think so.'

'You should *know.*'

'I suppose I have.'

Lily's flat was up three flights of rickety stairs, with the toilets on the landings. It was a sparsely furnished room with a table and bed and a broken-down old sofa. Next to this she had a small kitchenette where she did her cooking.

'I'm making toasted sandwiches,' she said. 'Do you want some?'

'No. I told you I was full up. But I'd like a cup of tea if you have it.'

'Sit down, Tam.'

I sat on the sofa. It was surprisingly comfortable, this surprising night. Lily was out of her coat and had kicked off her shoes, and she was very small, tiny almost. I sat with my legs apart while she was doing the cooking. It was lucky I had met her. This London was a lonely place, for all its crowds of people. When Lily came through from the kitchenette she was carrying a tray of toasted sandwiches and two cups of tea. She sat down beside me. Her bare, white legs. She was still wearing the short, tight working skirt, and I had a massive hard-on. It takes little to give you a hard-on when you are fourteen, and I had a *lot* to give me mine. But I was feeling awkward, sitting on that sofa.

'Do you take milk and sugar, Tam?'

I said I did and she asked how many sugars.

'Two spoonfuls.'

Lily stirred my tea, the milk and sugar. 'Aren't you going to drink it?'

'I feel a wee bit shaky.' The tray, with my tea on it, was sitting on her lap. 'I don't want to spill any.'

'But you want to drink it while it's still hot.'

'Give me a minute.'

'I'll give you all the time you want.' Lily smiled. 'I don't say *that* to too many guys.'

What a fumble, that cup of tea. I had to have spilled half of it, shaking the way I did. Her bare white legs and meaty thighs. I almost *burned* with the heat of her. My first night in London! It was like no night in my life. I doubt if I could have risen from that sofa and walked, I was so dizzy with excitement.

'Are you all right?' Lily feigned that she was concerned. 'Your face has gone all red.'

'I'm all right.'

She ate her toasted sandwiches.

'I'll make us both another cup of tea. I hope that you will be able to drink this one, Tam.'

I watched her rise with the tray and was rewarded a glimpse of white knickers. Lily, for all she was short, was trim and lithe and had a good arse on her. I tried to think of other things, of the street, the corners, how it would be in Glasgow. The news would be out that I had run away, and—for I was not unpopular—they would be wondering where I was. That, or McGuigan was already home and they would know I was in London.

It was really too bad about McGuigan, that he had been caught so soon. He had thirty pounds—why the fuck had he to try his hand at shoplifting? This was not the first time he had been caught law-breaking, and I fancied that he would be locked up by now.

When they asked about the thirty pounds, he could only say he had found it. But one sure thing: the police would have got out of him when he had last seen me. My mother, knowing her, would never be out of the police station, hoping they would find me alive and well. We had no phone—who had back then, in the Glasgow tenements?—and I intended to write, telling her not to worry. Edith, the rabbi's wife, had about summed it up right when she said she pitied her.

'Feeling better?' Lily asked.

'I am. A whole lot. I think I was only tired.'

Lily said that was good and she sat back down beside me. 'Take off your jacket, Tam.'

My legs felt weak, standing up and unzipping my jacket to take it off. 'Where will I sleep?'

'On the floor or in bed with me, it's up to you.'

'I have almost thirty pounds.'

'Where did *you* get thirty pounds?'

'McGuigan stole a wallet on the train and he halved the money.'

'That was good of him.'

'I'd have halved with him if it had been the other way round.'

'Do you miss McGuigan?'

'Not now, but I missed him today when I was on my own.'

'Why did you tell me about the thirty pounds?'

I felt my face flush. 'I don't know.'

'Was it to sleep with me?'

'It might have been.' I knew that she was teasing me, but there was nothing I could do about it. 'It's in my shoe,' I said.

'I put *my* money down my cleavage.'

'*Cleavage?*'

'Between my tits,' Lily said. 'Have you never heard of a cleavage?'

'No.' My hands were now much steadier and I was able to hold my cup and sip my tea. 'It must be a London word.'

'It is not.' Lily shook her head, a smile. 'They say cleavage back in Glasgow.'

'Well, I have never heard of it.' My cock was beginning to throb again. 'But it's good that you've a place to put your money.'

'All women do.'

'I use my shoe.'

'That's because you don't have tits.'

She had small, up-tilted ones. She must have changed her top, for her blouse was white and modest. But she was flaunting her legs, her thighs, and it was becoming a sort of torture. I had no idea what I should do and I was embarrassed by my erection, which could not have gone unseen.

'Do you want to see my money?'

'No,' she said, 'and I don't *want* your money.'

'I wasn't offering to give you it.'

'It sounded like you were.'

'I wasn't.' I would have given it to her, and she must have known that. 'But I like you, Lily.'

'Do you, Tam?'

'You know I do.'

'Because I've taken you home with me?'

'I think that you're dead nice.'

'Do you mean that you think that I'm attractive?'

'I do,' I said, 'but you're teasing me, Lily.'

'Have you ever been with a woman, Tam?'

'I've had a couple of feels, the lassies at the corner.'

'Is that all?'

'I've never been with a woman.'

★ * ★

Lily was bright in the morning. 'Wake up, Tam.'

It took a moment to remember where I was and what had happened during the night.

'I've the breakfast on,' she said, 'and I hope that you are hungry.'

I got out of bed. 'What time is it?'

'Almost eleven.'

My clothes were on the sofa, and I remembered the money in my shoe and hoped that it was still there.

'How do you feel?'

'I feel great.'

I had moved from the bed to the sofa stark naked. It was a strange, odd feeling, watching Lily.

'I'll wash your clothes for you,' she said, 'after we have eaten.'

I was suddenly worried as to the state of my under-pants. But when I looked for them they were not there.

'I've put them in the sink to steep,' she told me.

To steep! I pulled on my trousers. Lily was standing outside the kitchenette and you could smell the cooking. I could hardly look at her, thinking about my underpants.

'Do you like black pudding?'

I said I did, but I'd never felt so mortified, those soiled fucking underpants.

'What's wrong, Tam?'

'Nothing.' I was not about to say, about my under-pants. 'There's nothing wrong.'

She seemed to understand. 'I get shitty knickers, if I wear them long enough.'

'You do?'

'Of course. Everybody does, it's nothing to worry about.'

We ate our breakfast sitting on the sofa. Fried eggs and potato scones and black pudding. I was glad to see that there were no baked beans. Lily had changed into white slacks and a woollen jumper. I wore just my shirt and trousers, for she was steeping my socks and semmit too.

'You don't want to look like a vagabond.'

'How did you mean last night, *catch* something?'

'An infection. Gonorrhoea. But it can be easily cured with penicillin.'

'Do you think I have caught an infection?'

'I hope not.'

'I can't help it now anyhow, if I have.'

'Let's hope you haven't.' We had finished eating and were drinking tea. 'But I'll give you penicillin to take home with you, just in case.'

'I don't want to go home, Lily.'

'But you can't stay here, Tam. I would get into serious trouble if the law found out that you were here.'

Lily had washed off all her make-up and was looking much younger, fresher. A more wholesome appeal. She had grey-green eyes and a scar on her chin, where her boyfriend had hit her. 'He wore a big gold ring,' she said. 'I had to get seven stitches in.'

'How would the law find out that I was here?'

'People talk, and I've got neighbours. They would see you come in and out.'

'You could say I was your brother.' I had no intention of leaving Lily, not now, not after such a night with her. 'There's no one would question that.'

Lily dithered. 'We might get away with it for a few days, but that is all.'

'I'll go home after a few days.'

'Do you promise?'

'I promise.'

I made love with her again that afternoon, before she went to work. And I would continue to make love to her in the afternoons and again at night before I went home to Glasgow. She was my first love affair and the first woman I had seen completely naked, and I could not believe her beauty. I had her turn this way and that, to bend over, for it was all new to me, the wonder of her. My sweet love. I loved her lips and tits and round, smooth belly. She showed me how to make her come, touching on her clitoris. I adored her arse, the soft of it, and I could not get enough of her in the few days that we spent together.

Lily bought me shoes and shirts and two new pairs of jeans. I had worried that she would steal from *me*. When I asked her why she was buying for me, she shrugged and said she wanted to. 'I have no one else to buy stuff for.'

'I wish I could live my life with you.'

'But you can't. You're far too young. You'll need to go home, Tam.'

'I will go home, don't worry.'

'But I am worried. The cops could knock on the door at any time and they could do me for abduction.'

'What's abduction?'

'Two years in jail.'

'I wouldn't want you to go to jail.'

'Then you have to go home.'

I knew I would, but I did not want to leave her. 'Could you not come back to Glasgow with me?'

'I am in enough trouble as it is, without going back to Glasgow with you.'

'Will we meet again?'

'Not for a couple of years at least.'

This was my last night with Lily.

'I don't know what I'll tell my mother, when I get home.'

'Just don't tell her about *me.*'

'I'm not that daft, to tell her about you.' It had been agreed that I would go home the next day. 'I'm going to miss you, Lily.'

'I'll miss you too.'

The train left Euston at ten past twelve. Lily had bought a ticket for me, one-way to Glasgow. I can't say that I had seen too much of London, other than King's Cross. Lily's flat. The street where she lived. I remembered my first night with her, and how glad I had been to have a friend and then a lover. On the train I felt to cry, leaving Lily. There was a clock on the station platform and the train left right on time.

McGuigan was locked up in a remand home named Larchgrove when I arrived home. I thought that they had done him for London shoplifting but was soon to learn otherwise. McGuigan was held on a previous offence, a shop-breaking in Glasgow. When his case came up he was sentenced to two years' approved-school training. Wherever he went after that I do not know, for I did not see him again. But he was a good guy, high-spirited, and I did not blame him when I learned that he had told the cops we had been together. Had I been him the chances are I would have done the same.

I was arrested in Glasgow Central Station by two railroad police as I was walking from the train. After I was searched and questioned I was put in a holding cell. I expected my mother to come for me, to take me home and a 'speaking-to'. But rather than that, I was transferred to the custody of the Glasgow police and questioned by a detective.

'McGuigan has told us that you robbed a man on the train, going down to London.'

They expected me to tell them that McGuigan had robbed the man? This was an old police trick that I had heard about, that they get one to blame the other. I was not about to fall for it, and I did not think that McGuigan would have either.

'I don't know anything about a wallet.'

'That's not what McGuigan says.'

'I don't care what McGuigan says.'

'What did you *do* in London?'

'I walked about. It's a big place. There is plenty to see in London.' I sat at a desk opposite the detective. He wore a striped shirt and had beefy shoulders. 'What's all this about anyhow?'

'A stolen wallet.' He had a gold ring on one hand and a cigarette in the other. 'Why did you run away?'

'I was looking for adventure.'

'Did you find adventure?'

'I didn't steal no wallet.'

'How did you come by the shirts and pants?'

'I bought them.' Coming off of the train I had been carrying a small bag, containing the clothing that Lily had bought for me. 'There's no law against that, is there?'

'Where did you get the money to buy them?'

'I did some work on a building site.'

'I see.'

'You do?'

'That you're a fucking liar.' The cop leaned back in his chair. There was a small, barred window behind his head. 'We have your mother outside waiting for you.'

'Can I see her?'

'You can do what you want,' the cop said, standing up. 'We have nothing to hold you on.'

Looking back, I almost wish I had been held, to save

me meeting with my mother. This was to be the worst part of the whole thing—such a feeling of guilt, the misery I had put her through, and all the while not caring. I was caring in the police station, though, when I saw her tears and how old she looked, reaching out to me, her missing son.

'I was sure someone had done you in.'

'I won't run away again, Mammy.'

The police station was near to Gorbals Cross and we walked it home through the tenement streets. It was about two in the morning and they were all deserted, the tenements in darkness. My mother wore a brown coat and a white headscarf. I wanted to hold, to hug her, but—something in my upbringing—I could not do that. It would be too sissy. From the age of twelve or thereabouts I had ceased to touch my mother, for all I had wanted to. Despite my bad behaviour, I loved her very much, and never more than that night, when I had returned from London.

By November or December of our first year, Martin was a big pup. It had become my habit to buy him crisps when I went into a pub for a pint or two. The pubs we used were far from local. I had never had Martin in a pub where I was known, where there might be trouble. And I was careful too, when I was with him, that I was never the worse for drink. It was a good, high feeling to sit in a pub with my pal right there beside me.

We went into pubs in the daytime only, at the end of a walk. I had Martin on a choke chain now, which was the only way to handle him, to have full control. He was becoming incredibly strong and quick as a flash and I worried that he might break away from a normal lead and get himself run over. He was at that age, not one year old, when he could have easily got run over. Without a choke chain I do not know if I could have managed Martin.

Our pub visits were to come to a sudden stop. This was because of a one-eyed drunk I used to know. I had not seen this guy in twenty years, and I pretended not to notice him. But he noticed me with his one eye. I was reading a newspaper and he decided to surprise me. Which you should not do to a man who has a dog with him, and not to a man with a Doberman. My one-eyed friend could tell you that, for he almost lost his nose, and I would have lost Martin if he had lost his nose. And all because he was drunk and I was in the pub.

This was the first time I had seen ferocity in Martin.

He had always been so playful, a bundle of fun. But not that day in that pub. I had to fight to hold him back, away from the man behind me. Such a frenzy! On a blink. He had thought the man was attacking me and had reacted in his nature. Until then I had not thought that it was in his nature to behave like that. It had been a frightful transformation.

I did not tell my mother or sister about our adventure in the pub. They thought, the same as I had, that there was only love in Martin, and I wanted it to remain that way. My big pup. You always hear that it is the master's fault and not the dog's, when a dog gets into trouble, so when I heard about the Doberman Club I was not slow to take him there. To train me more than him, for there was more to Martin than I thought.

The Doberman Club was run by a strong-voiced ex-army man who brooked no nonsense. It was a serious business, his training school. He made that clear, and I was glad to hear it. I had not come to the Doberman Club for a social evening. It took an hour to walk there and an hour back again. We went once a week. I can't say that I liked the trainer but I was not there to like the trainer and I did not care if he disliked me. I was used to people disliking me.

The club was in a hall above a church and you had anything between fifteen and twenty Doberman pups at any one session. Martin was one of the older dogs, but he was far from being the biggest. There were some brutes of dogs, so-called pups, in that place. Martin liked it, but then he liked any place he was with me.

The trainer was good at his job, I'll say that for him. He knew dogs, the Doberman breed. He would demonstrate with his own dog what obedience should be. I had to admire him and his dog, the level they had achieved. When he told his dog to stay it stayed, not a movement, and it could stay like that—on its belly, on the floor—for the best part of a session.

I could not hope to equal that with Martin. But we were beginning to work together. He was picking up on me and I on him. The Doberman Club taught both of us that he had to do what I told him, when I told him.

There are no two Dobermans alike, I learned that too. The trainer's dog and Martin—well, I would doubt that even the trainer could have had Martin stay for half as long as his own dog did. It is all about the temperament of the individual dog. Martin was smaller than most, the other Dobermans; and he could never compete as a show dog: he was too small and had a rib too many. The vet had told me about Martin's extra rib when he was ill. I had not cared as long as he got better. What is an extra rib, a couple of inches? But there was never any question about his spirit. Martin was the boldest and the most faithful dog at the Doberman Club. Even the trainer remarked on how close he was to me. We attended weekly for several months, until he was not a pup any more and we had learned all that they could teach. Then we departed on good terms. This was the first in recent times that I left a place where people were without bad feelings.

That Christmas I went to Midnight Mass with my mother for the first time in many years. We sat in a front pew and we would sit in that same front pew for the next nine Christmases. I had no idea where I had been the Christmas before, but it could have been nowhere nearly so good as in the chapel with my mother and peace on earth and good will to all men.

I had known little peace for many years, but was nudging closer. A certain soothing in my heart, my soul? I had asked my mother to come with me to the chapel in a freezing late night. An odd thing: since Martin, I had become much closer to my mother. I was at home much more, for one thing. Before the arrival of my dog I had been given to disappearing. I could not do that now, with my new responsibility.

There were three priests on the altar saying the mass, and the altar boys, in their white vestments, were scrubbed so clean they looked pure and shining bright. My mother knew lots of people in the chapel and I knew that she was proud of me, that I was with her in the chapel. It had to be a minor miracle.

It was a good Christmas that Christmas, our first with Martin in the house, our new family member. He was not so wee now, but my mother was completely unafraid of him. Had she been afraid of him, Martin would have had to go. But rather than afraid, my mother was a fierce protector. She would let no one say a word against our dog. We had brought him up almost as a new child in the house.

He was a rebellious one at times. One night that Christmas he was sitting in my easy chair. When I tried to move him off, he did a bit of growling and showed me his teeth. The side incisors were a good inch long and sharp as razors. A touch from them could break your skin. I pointed to him. 'Off,' I said, but he only continued growling. Call me mad, but I found it touching, like he was trying for his self-respect, or that he had his right to be on the chair as I had mine. But I was surprised at this mutiny, and I put it down sharply. A shake of my fist, some harsh words. Martin got the message. His revolt passed over.

We exchanged gifts about two in the morning, my mother and sister and me. My sister had been minding Martin while my mother and I had been at Midnight Mass. A problem with Martin, he would howl for me when I went out. My sister did her best with him but she could not stop the howling. He had been up in my chair and looking out of the window, watching for me.

'Like a big wolf.'

'He must miss me.'

'You'll never find nobody who misses you more than he does.'

We had a coal fire and a Christmas tree, some Christmas decorations. I forget what gifts I got, but my mother treated Martin to a tin of Pal dog food. I remember that. He was usually fed a dried food that I mixed with water. It was good and nourishing and a fraction of the cost of tinned dog food. (Martin would have eaten six or seven tins of dog food a day and have still been wanting more.) My mother did not want Martin to feel out of things during the gift exchanging. And he had some memory, for the next Christmas and the next he would be looking for his tin of Pal dog food.

We went out that night, Martin and me. It had to be three in the morning. I was becoming a man of the open air, the open field. In stout walking boots and a hooded zipped-up jacket. It is easy to get pneumonia in Glasgow in the winter. A cold can lead to it. Or if you are simply run-down. I felt in robust good health. I was walking every day, and walking sometimes fifteen or even twenty miles. It is surprising how far you can walk when you are walking with a dog. I didn't think of miles or time, but the time flew in and the miles flew by. A man and his dog. It was a simple life, but it suited me, and Martin had to think that it would go on for ever.

We had snow in late January, which often happens in Glasgow. I forget the last time we had a white Christmas. The snow had begun in the night and it was really thick come morning. I had to visit the doctor about noon that day for a repeat prescription. It was not the first time I had been to the doctor's surgery with Martin. I was only inside for a couple of minutes and I tethered him outside. He would bark of course, and sometimes fiercely, as though urging me to hurry up.

Which I couldn't do, not that day. Inside the surgery, in the waiting room, a patient had taken a bad turn and the doctor was attending to her. I had to wait till this was over before I collected my prescription. When I did come out, the tethered Martin was being snowballed by a group of children who were across the street. He had been hit a few times, judging by the snow-marks on his head and body. While I can't say I liked the sport, could you call it that, I was willing to let it go—until, that is, he was struck by a heavy stone. I heard it thump against his ribs and he yelped out and I was over that street in a flash.

I had seen the boy who had thrown the stone. He was aged about twelve and was laughing madly at what he'd done, the pain he had inflicted. I am proud to say I paid him back in such a fashion that he would think twice before he stoned another dog again. He had one sore arse, that boy, when I was done with him. My swinging boot. I did not give a damn who was watching, and if his arse was sore so was my dog's ribs.

Martin's ribs hurt for a good week after, and that boy was really lucky that I only kicked his arse. I had to help Martin on to his couch that night. I was still angry. What had he done to that boy to have almost had a rib caved in?

It was that night, before I crossed to my bed and put out the light, that, as out of nowhere, I said, 'Good night, Martin.'

I would say it again the following night, and for years after, and with a profound sorrow on his last night.

That summer, I decided on a holiday. But where to go? Had I been alone I would have booked a package deal to Spain or Portugal, some place warm. But it was out of the question that I would go alone now that I had Martin. If I had put Martin in kennels I would have worried about him and not enjoyed the holiday. This is a very real drawback when you have a dog and are as close to him as I was close to Martin. You forfeit a fancied holiday. There are few hotels where dogs are welcome. It is, as I found out, hard to find accommodation for the two of you. Most places just don't want to know once they hear you have a dog. I phoned a couple of caravan parks in Scotland, but they would not have us. Finally, after several more calls, I got fixed up in a caravan in Bude in Cornwall.

It was a long way away and I was without a car. We had to go by bus; had we gone by train, Martin would have been caged up inside the guard's van. As it was he had never been on a bus before, not even a local one. I was concerned about the travelling.

It was six hours down to Birmingham, our first stop. The bus was only half full and we sat at the back. Martin seemed to sense my apprehension and was on his best behaviour. I began to feel at ease and—this was my first trip outside of Glasgow since I had been to London—I began to enjoy the journey.

We had an early start and got into Birmingham around noon. I had a canvas bag and tins of dog food and Martin got fed in Birmingham. I had his red plastic bowl and I had bottled his water back in Glasgow. So he had no complaints, I don't think, about our stop in the sun, in some park. I ate cheese sandwiches and drank a mug of coffee. I was becoming an expert in finding parks, empty spaces. We had three hours until the next bus to Cornwall and we spent it in the park.

It was dark when the bus drew up in Bude, which had an olde world feel about it. Martin sniffed the air and so did I. You could feel the change in climate. A warm, almost humid night. It begins to get cold in Glasgow in late August. But Bude was deep in Cornwall, many miles from Glasgow, and it was a velvet night. I had the key to our caravan and we set out to find the site. It felt wonderful to be out in the open air after hours on the bus. Martin had proven to be a great traveller, but he too had to be glad to be off of the bus, on his paws and trotting by my side. I had to ask for directions to the site from passers-by and, if I could barely understand them, or they me, it was all part of the fun, our adventure in another world.

The caravan park was a thirty-minute walk outside of town, but we found it easily. There was a big full moon to help us. Martin with his head up high, inquisitive to where he was. Not that he cared too much as long as I was with him. Had I been in Kathmandu he would still have followed me. His leader? Well, I was Batman and he was only Robin. But he was no Boy Wonder, not any more. Martin was a full-grown dog now. A sleek, hard seventy pounds in weight, at least. He had a tremendous chest and was thick at the shoulders, and if he was shorter than the standard Doberman he was much thicker, with a heavier and blunter muzzle and his extra rib. Martin had not been bred for show, that was obvious; I sometimes wondered about his lineage. It is possible that he had a bit of bull mastiff in him that had begun to out as he got older.

I could not have cared less. He was my pal and fate had flung us together, walking in the balmy night. There were only six caravans on the site and my key was for number five. You had to climb three steps to get inside. This was a first for me, a caravan. Inside it was surprisingly spacious, well laid out. We had two bedrooms and a lounge, a cooking area. I had booked the caravan for two weeks. It had been too long a journey to stay for one week, which I would have done if we had been in Scotland.

'This is it, Martin. The journey's end.' We were both sitting on the sofa. 'What do you make of it?' It had become the most natural thing for me to speak to him like that. 'We'll explore the place tomorrow.'

The caravan had cost only forty-five pounds for the two weeks, and Martin had travelled for free. So the holiday was cheap and something new for both of us.

We slept together, what else? Martin down at the foot of the bed. I forgot all about him after I put out the light. A smoke in bed. I rolled my own. A good thing about rolled-up cigarettes is that they go out if you fall asleep, which I had often done when I was drinking. There is every chance with a manufactured cigarette that you will alight the bed or, at the very least, burn your fingers badly. I had been rolling my own cigarettes since I was fifteen years old. While they could have done nothing for my health, at least I had escaped being burned.

★ * ★

The caravan door next to mine was opened, and a young woman began climbing down the steps from it.

'Have you just arrived?' she asked me.

'I arrived last night.'

'You sound Scottish?'

'I am Scottish.'

'What part of Scotland are you from?'

'Glasgow.'

'I have been in Edinburgh, but not Glasgow.'

'Most people who go to Scotland go to Edinburgh. It must be the castle.'

'Or Princes Street,' she said. 'The shops.'

'Where do you come from?'

'London. But I was born in Kingston in Jamaica.'

'My name is Thomas.'

'I'm Connie.'

I asked Connie if there was a nearby shop where I could buy some groceries.

'Do you need milk?'

'I do,' I said.

'I could have given you some.'

'I need a cereal too.'

Connie said that the shop was five minutes away and that she would show me to it.

'What is the name of your dog?'

'Martin.'

'I've never heard of a dog called Martin.'

'You have now.'

'Is he friendly?'

'I don't know.'

'*You* don't know?'

'He is when you get to know him.'

'Then I'd better not touch him until I get to know him.'

'I would like you to get to know him.'

Connie was in her mid-twenties. I had liked her straight away. Her manner and way, to say nothing of her looks.

'I'll show you to the shop,' she said.

Inside the shop I encountered a man with an Airedale dog. He wanted to talk—about dogs, of course—but Connie was waiting outside and I much preferred to speak to her. We had hit it off and I wanted to know all about her. I bought what groceries I thought to need, but I already knew what I needed most was *her*.

This was the first I had wanted a woman since I had Martin. Or perhaps with a bit more accuracy the first time I had *really* wanted a woman since I had him. It must have been. I had abstained from sex for the best part of two years. I could have been in a monastery as far as ladies were concerned. But it was all to change in Cornwall with Connie. We made love that same day, in my caravan.

I had been brought to my senses suddenly, with a black woman down in Cornwall. We had hardly beat about the bush when I had asked her inside my caravan, and I can remember our first kiss yet.

Connie was a financial adviser. She had been married once, but had no children. Since the break-up of her marriage she had lived alone. Recently, there had been some crisis in her life and she had come to the caravan park, she said, to chill out. It was the first I had heard this expression, to *chill out*.

Before she left the caravan we arranged to meet later that night—it was already night when she left me—and have a drink together. I thought Martin would sulk after she went, but I couldn't help that. I had found a wonderful woman, and I had been so long without a woman, it was exhilarating just to think of her and what we had done and would do again, and again. Connie had still one full week of her chill-out break to go.

I cooked a meal, but Martin would not eat. Did he feel betrayed? 'Suit yourself,' I told him. 'I've got to be considered too.'

And so I had. It was not that I was running out on him. I would never do that, but I could not sacrifice myself, not totally. I had denied myself enough. My last girlfriend, Tracy, had been a member of the Salvation Army. I had met her on a Glasgow street and we had fallen for each other. I used to meet Tracy two nights a week and a Sunday afternoon, after she had been to church. But I drank and she did not. Drinking is frowned on in the Army. I was something of a secret lover until, one Sunday, after I had been drinking all morning, I got fed up waiting for her and presented myself in church. This was madness. I stumbled in, and, when I was offered help, a cup of tea and some advice, I took offence and created a disturbance. Suffice to say, it was the end for me with Tracy.

That was nearly two years earlier, but I must have remembered it, for I refrained from drinking alcohol that night with Connie.

She drank white wine, a sip and a smile. All bright white teeth and liquid eyes, long slender fingers and her nails were painted silver. She looked very, very sexy. Not unlike a young Shirley Bassey, but blacker and more sturdy and with more heft at her arse and thighs. But the same appeal at the mouth and eyes, as though yearning for someone to hold and comfort her. It was the way it was with Connie and I loved her for it. She made me feel so much a man.

We sat back from the bar, and if I felt sorry for Martin, alone in a strange caravan, I could not help but feel glad for myself.

When Connie asked me what I did, I said I was a poet.

'Will you write a poem about us?'

I assured Connie that I would, when I got home.

'Have you written a poem about Martin?'

'No.'

'You should.'

'He couldn't read it.'

'You should still write it.'

'Do you think?'

'I know.'

'Then I might write it.'

'It could be a great poem.'

'I wouldn't go that far,' I said. I was beginning to feel a touch of a fraud, that I wasn't a poet at all. 'But it could be a good one.'

'What do you do for money, Thomas? You can't live off your poetry surely.'

'I'm on sick benefit.'

'What's wrong with you?'

'I'm antisocial.'

'That's all?'

'It is enough.'

'I don't think you are antisocial.'

'I couldn't be antisocial with you.'

'Then maybe you're recovering.'

'I'm not as bad now as I used to be.'

'Were you badly hurt?'

I said I was, had been. It was obvious that Connie had no idea about my problem. I had been hurt in love, that was how she thought, and it was better to let it go at that.

'Who was she?'

I invented a story of love and betrayal and how, at the end of it, I had distrusted everyone and would speak to no one and had been classed as antisocial.

'You got Martin then, when you were in that state?'

'He was the only one I thought I could trust.'

'What was your job before this happened?'

'I was working for the railway.'

'Will you go back to it when you have recovered?'

'I think that I might be recovered, Connie.'

No wonder I was antisocial, all of that. One lie running to another. I should have told Connie that I was an electrician or some such job. It would have been more simple, straightforward. But I had been caught off guard. Why had I claimed to be a poet? I had published a few short stories, but I was no poet and would never be a poet.

The lie made neither rhyme nor reason. I suppose I knew she would disappear out of my life as quickly as she had come into it.

I had a delightful week with Connie. We got on together and the sex was great. But it was an interlude, no more, and at the end of the week she went back to London. Once again it was only me and Martin. I think, if I don't know how, that after a time he had caught on that I had needed Connie.

I had Connie's address in London, but I did not contact her. Likewise, she had my address in Glasgow, but she did not contact me. Two strangers in a caravan park. I would imagine that we both knew better than to try to keep it going, what we had shared. There are some things, and this was one, that cannot be repeated. You have no choice but to let it go, which we did.

Together again, just the two of us; Martin was delighted. Why not? It must have seemed for him that I had been a missing party while I was with Connie. She had been a part of my holiday. A man must live, and I felt the better for having been with her.

But it was good to be back again with Martin. My old pal. He was only some eighteen months old, but I thought of him as an old pal. He was the only pal I ever had who had gone that distance, eighteen months.

We had explored nothing and I set about to put that right by way of a local map. It showed close up where we were and, rather than walking to no place, I would target a town for us to visit. A day trip. Anything up to ten miles there and ten miles back was okay for me, for us.

I had to sometimes collar Martin, especially where there were sheep about, but usually he was off the lead and trotting behind or just in front of me. I tried to keep to paths and open fields. It was as well that I have a good sense of direction. It was sometimes three or even four hours before we reached our destination, but we always got there. Two weary travellers. We deserved our food and drink. I had discovered a new tinned dog food called Chappie. It was cheaper than the other brands and you could buy huge tins of it, and Martin liked his Chappie. I carried it in a haversack, together with his bowl and a bottle of his water. There was usually a bakery in the town, where I would buy my food. I had a flask to make coffee with. We would sit on a bench and both tuck in. When it was time to go back to our caravan Martin would lead the way. It did not matter how far we'd gone, he always knew the way back. This was more than helpful, for it was almost always dark by then and I was none too sure of the way myself. Starlit nights, but had I been alone I could have easily got lost.

I enjoyed my last week in Cornwall with Martin as much as I had enjoyed my first week there with Connie.

Well, almost.

Going home, we arrived in Birmingham in the afternoon, but it was a long stopover; we had to hang around for the night bus back to Glasgow. It was a fine, warm day and about seven o'clock that night we were sitting in a park when a thick, strong-looking guy sat right down beside me. I did not like the look of him, and I liked the look of his dog even less. It was a brindle-coloured bull terrier. I could tell by the look and the talk of this guy that he was something of a tough nut. Or he thought he was. There is a huge difference. A lot of *really* tough guys are quiet and softly spoken.

Martin was playing in bushes behind where we sat. My companion wore a dirty T-shirt and his arms were covered with tattoos. He had his dog on a long chain lead and he told me that his name was Brutus. It looked the part, did Brutus: a true brute, much the same as his master. He went on to tell me that Brutus had killed two large German shepherd dogs. When he told me this he had unleashed Brutus. What the fuck! Did he intend that Martin would be his dog's third kill?

I was up on my feet and into the bushes, but the fight was already on. A fierce one. Brutus had his teeth in Martin's chest, just beneath his throat. They were whirling round and round, and Martin, he was much the taller, had his head in the air and his eyes bulged out and had a queer blue light that I had never seen before. The tattooed guy looked up at me and shook his head as if, because of Brutus's grip, the fight was as good as over.

I was powerless to stop this fight, for they were moving far too quickly. But a new turn came and Martin somehow shook free of Brutus's grip. I could see the bloodstains on his chest. Brutus was panting heavily, but he must have smelled the blood, for he flung himself on Martin. I thought it was the end of Martin, I truly did. The frenzied Brutus was up in the air, all four of his paws off of the ground, the quicker to get at my dog. Martin stood sort of sideways, crouching. He did not deserve to come to this, but there was still nothing I could do. I could have lost a hand, or both my hands, in this fight had I tried to interfere. Both dogs were gone, totally out of control; Martin as much as Brutus. He had been getting the worst of it till now, but he was still there on his own four paws. One thing about Martin, he had heart. A raw courage. Brutus was a bully dog, bred for fighting. It was all he knew, all he could do. God only knows the fights he had been in. Fights his tattooed master had bred him for. Had Martin lost I think I would have killed him. He had, without my knowing, set his dog on Martin. An unequal contest, or so he had thought. With Martin fighting for his life, I felt my head spin with rage.

The flying Brutus had a rat-like tail and a big, blunt snout. The crouching Martin had his head down, but you could see his teeth and he was watching Brutus. At the peak of his leap, Brutus had to have been three foot in the air. Or even closer to four. He thought to land on Martin's back? Brutus had to weigh about sixty pounds and he would have buckled Martin under him if he had landed on his back.

I would have tried to kick him off if that had happened. But I would have needed to be in there quickly, to save Martin before Brutus chewed his head off.

This whole happening was awful, the crazed bulldog

and his loony owner. Then another new turn in the fight. Brutus had fallen short in his jump and Martin had him by the throat. Martin, in a planted stance, stood over a downed Brutus, and you could see the muscles in Martin's back and neck working his head from side to side.

'Hey! He cost me 400 pounds,' the man yelled.

I hit him full on the mouth with a right-hand punch. He had some real teeth and a metal bridge and they all smashed out and he was out, unconscious. Sprawled on some low bushes. I put the choke chain on Martin and managed to pull him away from Brutus. Not without a struggle, though. He had tasted blood and wanted more from the dead or dying Brutus.

My fist hurt. I did not know it then, but I had a tooth embedded in a knuckle. When I returned to Glasgow I had it removed in the emergency ward in the Victoria Hospital. My hand had swollen to twice its size and poison had set in. I was put on penicillin for a couple of weeks afterwards.

In the park in Birmingham it took a time for Martin to calm down to something like his normal self, to be able to take him on the bus. In his bloody chest there were four holes and his fur was ripped. But he had survived. I bandaged him up with shirts of mine and could only hope that he would make the journey.

When the bus arrived in Glasgow we took a taxi home and I took him to a vet that same morning. The vet told me that I was lucky to still have Martin. The tooth holes in his chest—another couple of millimetres and they would have pierced his heart.

'Was it a pit bull terrier he encountered?'

'I don't know about a pit, but it was a big bull terrier.'

'Probably a pit.'

Martin was up on a table and I held his head while the vet put stitches in his chest. I was given pills to give to him, for pain. 'He'll be sore for a few days yet.'

An inexpensive holiday? Not after I had paid the vet. I had thought for twenty or thirty pounds, but the treatment cost a hundred.

The time rolled on and the days drew short and Guy Fawke's Night and Halloween arrived, and then it was December. Christmas trees and fairy lights. I teased Martin with balloons. He would paw them down, out of the air, with an almost cat-like movement. I kept to myself what had happened with Brutus. To explain Martin's injuries, I said he had become entangled with barbed wire. It was as good an excuse as I could think up. Aside from his injuries, Martin was unchanged. He was still playful with other dogs, if a little aloof; but he had always been aloof and happy just to be with me. We were two of a kind in many ways, Martin and myself.

As Christmas grew near, I prepared to attend another Midnight Mass with my mother. I was never big on religion and it was the only mass that I attended. According to my mother, it was the only mass that many a member of the congregation attended. I would be forty-two come February and you can't fight time and it would be silly to say that I was a stronger man than I had been five years before. But it is a definite fact that I was a *better* one and all-round fitter for my age.

My first full year with Martin. Christmas to Christmas. In the chapel with my mother I recognized the priests on the altar from the year before. This oasis of good will. Decency. Christian love. *Love one another as I have loved you.* Some hope! But it did no harm to pretend for the duration of the Midnight Mass.

My father had believed it all: the teachings of the Catholic Church, the Pope's infallibility, plenary indulgences, whatever they are. He used to go to novenas and the Stations of the Cross, and he fasted on Good Friday.

Sadly, I did not share his faith, and neither did my mother, not really. Chapel was more a meeting place for her than a house of prayer. She would look around for people she knew and point them out to me. We would crack jokes about them and the priests. I can be funny and my mother could be funny too, and we were entertained in chapel.

I think that religion should be fun, and fun it was for us. I had often to suppress my laughter. My mother would pretend to be angry with me, but she was almost laughing too. My snide remarks about the priests and some people in the congregation, they did no harm. My jokes were too stupid to do any harm. I did not know the priests nor a soul in the congregation.

Not that, despite all our secret jokes, my mother was a non-believer. Far from it. She believed all right, but was without my father's fervour. How he had prayed! There would have been no joking in the chapel had my father still been with us.

In many a way my mother retained a girlish streak and many a time I would treat her like a little sister. I know she had despaired for me, and *herself,* because she thought I would be murdered. Or that I would murder someone and go to prison. Martin had changed all that. I did not now mix with the sort of men I had mixed with in the past.

That part of my life was over. I did not miss it, and I would doubt that those men missed me and my brooding ways. I was never good company in a pub; *I* would not have drunk with me.

Martin was given his Christmas treat, his tin of Pal. I had treated my mother and sister to a meal about a week before, for their Christmas, and we had exchanged gifts then. They were never anything big, more like token gestures. Half of the time in my former life I had missed it altogether, Christmas and New Year. The *bells.* You have people who seldom drink drinking then. Not me, though. I might watch the parties on television, but there would be no drinking. My night in the field in the summer was the last time I had drunk. None of the people at *those* New Year parties would end up sleeping in a field. But more than that, I did not want to drink. I valued peace and the simple life, out walking with my dog.

I was back with Tracy, the Salvation Army girl I had lost through drink. Things were good. I had waited for Tracy to come out from church. It had been a cold, wet night and at first she would not speak to me, a repentant lover, standing with my dog.

'I don't drink now,' I said.

Tracy said nothing, walking on in her Army coat and flat, black shoes, wearing her little round hat.

'Say something to me, Tracy.'

But still nothing. She was haughty—still smarting from my behaviour in the church that horrible Sunday, when I had been mistaken for a beggar, a homeless man, and had lashed out. I could blush myself when I thought about it— those strict teetotallers, and how Tracy had been in tears.

'I think I might have seen the light,' I said, walking in step with Tracy. I had been out of her life for two full years. Was this madness? Not for the first time it crossed my mind that she could be married, or even a mother now. 'Are you, Tracy?'

'Am I what?'

'Married?'

'No.' She was still walking, but slower now. 'Are *you*?'

'No.' I wanted to hold her. 'I've missed you like crazy, Tracy.'

'Only now? It's been two whole years.'

'I couldn't face you until now.'

Tracy's eyes were blue, but they looked black in the night. In the light, under her little round hat. It looked to be soaked, heavy with rain. Martin was soaked too, and so was I, and we were standing now, the three of us.

'You could have said that you were sorry,' Tracy said.

'I am saying it now, that I am sorry.'

'Two years on.'

'I've never stopped thinking about you.'

'I should tell you to piss off.'

'Do you want me to?'

'You know I don't.'

I did? She looked at Martin.

'I didn't take you for a dog man, Thomas.'

'His name is Martin.'

'That's a strange name for a dog.'

'It's a stranger story how I came by him.'

'Have you really stopped drinking?'

I assured her I had. 'What happened before won't happen again.'

Tracy asked for time to think before meeting me again.

'Sure,' I said. 'Take all the time you need.'

Prior to Connie I had peace of mind, just me and Martin. I had begun to think that I could live without women. But after Connie I thought about women all the time, and Tracy in particular. There might be a warning here, in this, for any young priest who thinks *just once.* Forget it. The chances are it will go to three or four and more. My own celibacy had been more to do with a lack of opportunity than any self-denial. My desire had gone, until I had met

Connie. A lustful reawakening that would not subside, not a bit, and I was in as bad a way as when I was fourteen years old. Which might have been all right then, but was all wrong now. Most men of my age were married and had families. Some guys I had gone to school with were already grandfathers. I walked the fields with a big black dog and—a first time with Martin—a feeling of discontent. A sense that there was more to life than this dull existence. From a public pest I had become a virtual hermit.

I gave Tracy a week before I resumed my quest for her. I wanted her madly, if, inside, I was beginning to wonder if it had been too long. Could we rekindle what used to be? I had to try. I met her coming back from church a week later. Martin knew her now and he was friendly, sniffing up against her.

'What's the verdict, Tracy?'

'We'll give it a try,' she told me.

I had an odd adventure in a toilet in a public park one Sunday. I used to wait inside this park for Tracy until after her Army service. It was a vantage point and I could see her coming from a long way off. On the main road that ran adjacent to the park. I would then meet with her and walk her home, but that was all, for I had Martin with me.

Martin was the reason I was *in* the park.

It was an ice-cold day. A high red sun and skeletal trees. The grass was stiff and white with frost and it crunched beneath your feet. I can remember that day with a rare clarity. How cold it was. The high red sun and I could have been in Russia. In Siberia. You get days like that in Scotland, real freezers. Martin ran in front of me, straight into a public toilet. A sign said "Gents." And there were a few gents inside that place, as I soon found out.

This was one of the few times in my life when I have been totally naïve. The toilet was at the end of a narrow path between high hedging. Martin appeared to pause at the entrance, as though he was waiting for me, and, knowing him, I knew there was something wrong. Inside the toilet. I thought perhaps, on such a day, some frozen tramp. Martin began to growl and I began to hurry. Towards the toilet. It was painted white and had the look of a small cottage. A man appeared to emerge from it. He was blocked by Martin. At the entrance. He then vanished back inside the toilet, Martin was guarding the front, the door. What had that man been up to? In the park inside the toilet on this cold day? I had no option—the insistent Martin; for he would not leave his post—but to investigate.

One man? There had to be twenty men inside that toilet. I had never seen anything like it, and Martin went berserk. He thought two men were one strange beast that he had not seen before? I certainly had not. The one guy on his hands and knees and both of them with their trousers down, bare-arsed in the toilet.

I have to say they were an alarming sight and Martin bit a chunk of the top guy's arse.

There were teenage boys and older men, some of them half undressed.

We were all, those men and me, in a state of shock, this happening.

Martin, as a wild thing, out of control, running amok, biting at anything that moved. One man chanced a kick at him. I heard the thud. He was a big red-faced fellow. Had he kicked again I would have chinned him. There was nobody kicking my dog twice. This wild melee! There were howls and screams and it was just as well the park outside was empty. I kept my eye on the red-faced guy, for I was on Martin's side. An us-against-them sort of thing. Another try for a kick from him and I would have been in there swinging.

Martin was in there biting. He was up in the air and down again and there were hospital cases for sure; the man with the chunk bitten out of his arse. Not that I was caring, not about him or them. My concern was for Martin. When the place had cleared I managed to get the lead on him and we made it away before the cops arrived.

There was a piece about this in a local newspaper, *dog runs amok in a public convenience.* The police were looking for a big black dog and a burly man. They had not to look very far, but no one came knocking at my door.

Tracy was into good works, one of which was helping out in a soup kitchen in Glasgow city centre. She did this twice a week, on Monday and Thursday nights. In the weeks that followed, I tried to visit her at least one of those nights each week, with Martin. Tracy was quite fond of Martin and he would get a roll and sausage. It made his night, and she made mine. How good she looked in her uniform.

The soup kitchen catered for bums and tramps and worn-out old prostitutes. They were all welcome for a mug of tea and a bite to eat. The Salvation Army are trying their best to help the unfortunates of this world. One of whom, I was surprised to see one night, was an old girlfriend of mine—no, more than that, she had been my *first* girlfriend. When I was fourteen I had thought to love her. We had lived in the same street, Maggie and I, in the old slumland Gorbals. I had not seen her for many years—since, I think, I was sixteen—but I knew her straight away.

She was a couple of years older than I was, which would have made her forty-four. She looked more like sixty-six. But something about her, at the mouth, her eyes, the way she stood, very much the same old Maggie, the girl who I had known. She'd once been full of devilment, teasing all the boys and me. Especially me. She had known how I felt about her and outside a tenement close one night she had asked me if I loved her. I had told her plainly that I loved her more than anything. But she had said she'd been with other guys, and when I said that didn't bother me, she hushed me and said she was in love with another guy and that they were leaving soon for London.

'When?'

'Soon.'

'I'll miss you.'

'There's lots of other lassies.'

And so there were. But then, for me, in that place, there had been only Maggie. I later heard she had become a prostitute. By the looks of things at the soup kitchen, she was still one. She recognized me as surely as I did her: 'Don't say it.'

'Say what?'

'That it's been a long time.'

'Twenty-five years at least,' I said.

'How are you, Tam?'

'Much the same, I think,' I said.

'You can't be much the same,' she said, 'not after all that time.'

'I'm okay.'

Maggie was eating a sausage roll, and she appeared relaxed and unconcerned. Was she used to this, meeting guys she used to know?

'You look okay.'

'So do you.'

'Who do you think you're kidding, Tam?'

'You're still you.'

'What are you doing here?' she asked. 'You're not looking for business, are you?'

'I'm walking the dog.'

'Come off it.'

'I go with one of the girls who runs this place.'

'Then she must be a member of the Sally Ann.'

That's what some people called the Salvation Army, whether with affection or not I don't know.

'She is,' I said. 'What's wrong with that?'

'Are you?'

'No, I'm not a member of the Sally Ann.'

'Then how come you're going with her? I thought that members of the Sally Ann went with other members of the Sally Ann.'

Maggie stood in a short red coat and a too-tight skirt that emphasized her belly.

'Have you been married?' she asked me.

'No.'

'Never?'

I shook my head.

'I have.' Maggie finished her sausage roll and licked her fingers. Her nails were bitten to the quick and her hands were fat and podgy. *She* was fat and podgy in her too-tight skirt and high-heeled shoes. 'Two times. They were both bastards,' she said, and walked off without saying a goodbye.

Tracy had seen us speaking, and asked me who she was.

'A girl I used to know,' I said, 'when she was young and so was I.'

Not long after this, Tracy and I called it a day. There was nothing dramatic about our splitting up this time. It might have been that we tried too hard, for it was never on. Not really. Not for either one of us and we both knew that. What had been was gone for ever. Something was not there; whatever *that* is. I think we had both known from the very beginning that it would not work, that we both had changed, and better to let go then than to drag it on to what could have been a bitter end.

I went back to Bude with Martin in the early spring. We travelled down the same way as before, with a stop in Birmingham. The chief difference this time was that I had a beer and whisky while waiting for the change of coach. That one beer and one whisky was enough to cause an almighty craving for more booze. I have often wondered if a heroin addict craved as desperately for his fix as I craved for alcohol on that trip to Bude. We were booked into the same caravan park and, when we alighted from the coach in Bude, Martin knew his way. He could have taken *me* to the caravan park. But I was thirsting for another drink and stopped at the Long John Silver, the pub I'd first visited with Connie. I drank at least five pints of cider and a couple more whiskies. Martin sat at my feet. This drinking was much more for need than for enjoyment. You can sometimes get away with a first drink, but if you are alcoholic, most likely you won't. I didn't, not that time.

When I arrived at the caravan park I had a clinking bag of scrumpy, which is a rough sort of cider. The slogan on the bottles read LEGLESS BUT HAPPY, and there was a drawing of a man with a drunkard's nose and the most stupid grin. He was out cold, propped up against a wall. This did not worry me one bit and I proceeded to drink the scrumpy. It was a flat, still brew and there were bits of apples floating in it. I downed four or five bottles and then went out for a walk with Martin. I remember locking the caravan door, but that is all I can remember of that night. I woke the following morning on a grassy slope beside a brook. The noise of the water hurt my head. It was eleven o'clock and the sun was high and it was already warm. Martin began to lick my face. I had a stubble of a beard and felt like Rip Van Winkle. After my long sleep, I had no idea where we were, but I thought we were in Cornwall. That was all, just *thought*. It was an effort to rise, and I wished that I was at home in bed. I would have gone back to sleep if I was back home, in a darkened room. My thumping head, the hot sun. Martin was without his lead, and when I began to look for it, in the grass, I discovered one full bottle of scrumpy. There were two more empty bottles that I must have drunk but could not remember drinking. Still, the place was quiet and I was almost sure that I had gone unseen, my party in the night. It was far from a party now.

I should not have drunk in Birmingham. It was Birmingham that had led to this, me in the grass above a brook, drinking down still more scrumpy. I cracked open the bottle, its tin-top cap, and all but downed it in one swallow. Martin looked up at me. He recognized booze and I thought I could see his disapproval. Whoever had designed the label on the scrumpy bottle had not been kidding about the legless bit. I had never known a brew to have me out the way it had. But I was feeling much better, more focused, for the one remaining bottle. It helped to put things in perspective, that a night in the open was no disaster.

'At least it did not rain,' I said to Martin. 'And no one will know but us.'

On our way back to the caravan I stopped for a drink

in the Long John Silver. Some three or four pints of *normal* cider. The pub was busy with tourists and some local fishermen. I began to think about my money and how much I had already spent. It had to amount to a pretty penny, the drink I had consumed. *Would* consume, for I was without an option now. I had some bodily need to drink again. I was far from home and it was frightening. At the very best I could only hope that Martin and me would make our way safely home to Glasgow. I said a prayer to that effect, in the Long John Silver.

I remember little of the next few days of our holiday in Bude. I was back on the scrumpy, not eating, forgetting to feed Martin. I thought only of my next drink and where it was coming from. And with reason, for my funds were insufficient to maintain a drinking binge.

Not too far from the Long John Silver I had noticed a wishing well, a round, old stone structure. The custom was that you threw some coins into it. There was a metal grating to protect the money from being stolen. This grating had a single padlock that could easily be jemmied. At the bottom of the well was about a foot of water and a hoard of coins. On our first or second day in Bude I had wandered across to the well with Martin in complete innocence. There were a lot of one-pound coins in it, in the water beneath the grating, but I could only look and wish that they were in my pocket.

I had become something of a regular in the Long John Silver in the mornings, when, to look at anyhow, I was not too drunk. Martin would be seated at my feet. I was on nodding terms with the fishermen, but we kept to ourselves, myself and Martin. He had to be worried about his master. We had been together for a long time now and he did not want to lose me. I did not want to lose him either; but such is the way of the alcoholic, I was prepared to take the chance.

When I left the Long John Silver, about one in the day and sometimes sooner, I would head for the shop that sold the scrumpy. It was not expensive, but bottle after bottle it added up. At the end of my first week in Bude, I had little money left.

'There is only one thing for it,' I told Martin that night. 'Let's hope that we don't get caught.'

We stole out from the caravan, Martin and me, in the early hours. I had cut down on booze all that day and was relatively sober. Walking Martin on his choke chain, I had a small but heavy jemmy that I had acquired from outside a plumber's yard. It would do the trick, no problem. I wore white trainers, wishing they were black, and we set a brisk pace into town.

'You stand guard,' I told Martin.

He just looked up at me.

It was a surprisingly light, bright night and I could see the coins clearly under the water below the grating. I jerked with the jemmy and the padlock snapped off and clanged down on the grating. I paused to look around, for it had sounded loud, that clanging, to me.

'Keep a lookout, Martin.'

The grating was awkward to lift, but I managed it somehow. It came away in two parts. I lifted out only one of them. Martin watched me intently. The night was cool but I felt hot, and there was sweat on my brow from my efforts with the grating. I was over the wall and half in the well, pulling out the grating. This wishing-well robbing was not so easy as I had thought it would be. I'd expected to jemmy the padlock and be in the money in short order. Not this stubborn grating. I had to have been at that grating for a good ten or fifteen minutes, trying to get a hold of it and lift the one half out. It was a cunning device, with holes big enough for coins but not quite large enough for fingers. Finally I got it off.

I removed my shoes—I wore no socks, for I had been expecting this—and rolled up my trouser bottoms. A paddle in the money. It had not been easy to get at, but it was worth it now, for such a thrill, scooping up the coins.

I had scooped a few when Martin began to low-growl. His ruff was up and I stepped out of the well and put the lead on him. Which was just as well, for, out from the shadows, a policeman appeared. He was wheeling a bicycle.

'What do you think you are doing?'

I was standing in my bare feet, my trouser legs still rolled up. Martin strained at his lead and he was all for going for the cop.

'Keep that dog away from me!'

The cop had stopped well short of us. It was only me and him and Martin. What to do to get out of this? I had been caught bang to rights. The cop stood with his bike in one hand and his helmet in the other. Martin was still low-growling, baring his teeth; when he was like that he was very, very frightening.

'The dog is my pal and if I go to jail he will be taken away from me.' The cop was a skinny, young guy. 'Give me a break, will you?'

'You are Scottish?'

'Glasgow.'

'You should be in cuffs,' he said in a tough voice. But I sensed that the cop was dithering. You don't meet too many too-brave guys in this world.

'I've got a pocket full of one-pound coins.'

The cop looked round him. What a quandary. He did not know what I might do. Nor did I for that matter. But we were both aware of Martin, what *he* would do. Was arresting me, or trying to, worth some fingers or a hand, an arm?

'Put some of the coins on the ground and walk away,' he told me. 'If you do that we will call it quits and you won't hear no more about it.'

I did as he said, and so did he.

That night was the closest I would ever come to losing Martin. Had it been a different, more reckless policeman, I would have been in jail and Martin would have been in the dog pound. Eventually—for first there would have been a fight, I'm almost sure. I was not about to just *let* them take my dog away. What the cop with the bicycle must have seen. It was a harrowing adventure, but there was a bus departing from Bude to Birmingham at six that morning and we were on it. I paid my fare with one-pound coins.

When we arrived in Birmingham I went back to the pub where I had been before and again I paid with one-pound coins. I do not know if the cop handed in his share, and it had nothing to do with me anyhow what he did. He had let us go and I will always be grateful to him for that. Perhaps it was the prayer I said in the Long John Silver, when we had first arrived in Bude. There is no telling, but we should not have got away with it, and I can only think that it was the prayer I said that saved us.

The following year, in early November, I went to Hexham, in Northumberland, with Martin and my sister. She had asked to come along. A broken romance or something? So we set out, the three of us. She had no problem with Martin, and the caravan had two rooms.

Hexham was no distance in comparison to Bude. The first stage was a bus to Edinburgh, then on to Berwick, which is just over the border into England. From there we got a local bus to Hexham. In all, a journey of about three and a half to four hours. We arrived in Hexham at about three o'clock.

It was a fine, bright day and the caravan was sited about six miles out of town. We decided to walk to it. I had Martin on his lead and he loved this. We were going adventuring. I hoped for no such adventure as we had had in Birmingham. I had been jumping out of my skin in Birmingham. It was, far and away, the biggest fright I had had with Martin.

Since that fight I had kept Martin away from all bull-breed dogs. Not that we would encounter another Brutus, but there is no point in courting danger. On the way to our caravan—it seemed a long six miles—my sister asked if I knew where I was going.

'Martin knows.'

'Be serious.'

'I know where I'm going.' I had been given instructions over the phone, where the caravan was from Hexham. 'We'll find it, don't worry.'

But I *was* worried. We had been walking for the best part of three hours and it should not take three hours to walk six miles. I had to have taken a wrong turn. One road looked much like another and they were all flat, with high, wild hedging at the sides. There was no one walking and no traffic. We had bags to carry and the day was closing and the bags were weighing and some first stars were showing. Not the best start to our holiday. I was beginning to think we might need to sleep in the open, under a hedge or in a haystack. Martin seemed to sense that we were lost and stuck the closer to me.

It was fully night when we came to a house that had a

lighted upstairs window. It was a gloomy-looking sort of place, forbidding. But we needed help to find our way and that house was our only immediate hope. Still, I was apprehensive about disturbing the owner. It looked damned creepy, lonely and imposing. Just the one light on in the upstairs window. My sister hung back a little as I rang the front doorbell. There was no answer. I rang again, and again there was no answer. I looked at Mary, she looked at me. Martin had nudged in close and I could feel his head against my thigh. It had become quite cold. What to do? I rang on the doorbell one more time. The house was not empty. I had seen the light in the upstairs window. But whoever had been in that room was not coming to the door of this bleak house.

'We had better go,' I told my sister.

'The light has gone out,' she told me.

'It has?'

'Look for yourself.'

We walked back from the house towards the road. I *knew* we were being watched, eyes behind the curtains. I had Martin on his lead, the choke chain. Where was the fucking caravan? I had the name of a pub where it was supposed to be near, but this was too forlorn a place for any pub to be.

'We should find a phone box and phone the pub,' Mary said, and I wondered why I had not thought of that before, for we had passed a few phone boxes. 'We could ask them to get a taxi for us.'

This was our first good thinking of the night, but before we could find a telephone box a police car pulled up beside us. Two uniform cops got out of it and we had flashlights in our faces. Martin jerked against his lead, ready to attack.

'What are you doing here?' one asked.

'We're looking for a caravan.'

'You won't find one in Catherine Cookson's house.'

'That's Catherine Cookson, the *writer's* house?' Mary asked with more than a little awe in her voice. She was a big fan of Catherine Cookson's books.

'Aye,' said the cop. He had a thick Geordie accent. 'That's her house and she don't like prowlers.'

'We're not prowlers.'

'What are you doing at her front door, then?'

'We were lost and wanted to ask for directions.'

'You thought *she* would direct you?'

'We didn't know whose house it was.'

My sister said, 'We can knock on a door if we want to. There is no law against knocking on a door, is there?'

'What about this caravan?'

'It's beside the Lion pub,' I said.

Martin was low-growling and the cops stood well away from him. The flashlights were not in our faces now, but these cops, a distrustful two, were not about to let us go until they checked our story out. One cop went back to the car to radio into the police station.

'Where is this pub?' Mary asked the other one.

'A couple of miles down the road.'

Martin was still low-growling.

'What kind of dog is that?'

'A Doberman.'

Mary asked whether we had alarmed Catherine Cookson, who, I have no doubt, was still peering through the curtains.

'She's not used to strangers,' the cop said.

'I'm not surprised,' I said, looking back at the house.

'She could charge you with trespassing.'

'For knocking on her door?'

'It's private property.'

I let that go and hoped that Catherine Cookson would too.

The first cop returned from the police car.

'Are you a Mr Thomas Healy?'

I said I was. The cop told us that the guy in the pub, who owned the caravan, was wondering where we were.

'I have already told you, we got lost.'

'We're *still* lost,' Mary said.

'We'll take you there.'

'You must be joking,' the second cop told his mate. 'We'll take the lass, but him and his dog can walk.'

My sister said that she'd walk too if they couldn't take the three of us. We were given directions by the cops and, alone again, the three of us set out to find the caravan.

What a relief to see the Lion pub! It was all lit up in the country dark. I wondered how we had missed it. We must have walked around it many times, going no place. I had been so *sure* to have known the way when we had been in Hexham.

'Where did you get to?' the pub owner asked us.

'Catherine Cookson's house.'

'We got lost,' Mary said. 'I think that we have been walking round in circles.'

At the bar in the Lion pub, our caravan was almost outside, just across a cobbled forecourt. Our host had two Jack Russell terriers. They were lively little dogs and he went hunting with them. Martin would be at home in this pub. I would find out later that it attracted dog owners from all around the district. On any one night you might encounter as many dogs as people. I was told that there had never been a dog fight, and I intended it to stay that way. A *good* Martin. I would have been mortified had he broken the peace, this haven for dogs and for dog people.

Back in Glasgow, I was now attending Sunday mass at night-time with my mother. It began at seven and we were home by eight. The parish priest was Father Reilly. He was a thin, white-haired man who smoked a pipe. I had met the Father once before, in a field, where he had been with his dog, a handsome golden Labrador. He was dressed in a white shirt and a black leather jacket and I had not known he was a priest. We passed some words and went our way and the next I saw of him he was on the altar at Midnight Mass.

Father Reilly was running a film show of Lourdes, where he had often been. My mother asked if I would go with her to the chapel hall to view it. The show was on one night a week for five weeks. Father Reilly featured in the films and did the commentary. The idea was to drum up support from the parish for a pilgrimage to Lourdes. My mother had no intention of going to Lourdes, but she enjoyed the film show and listening to Father Reilly. So did I. He had a quiet, charismatic way and he almost had *me* with him on his pilgrimage to Lourdes.

Outside of myself and Father Reilly, the gathering was female. I would think about thirty women. We got together at the interval for tea and cookies, and one night Father Reilly let it slip that he had once been a drinking man. 'A bottle of whisky a day and often more,' he said. But he was now a Pioneer. I asked him what a Pioneer was.

'It is a person who has taken a pledge to the Sacred Heart not to drink for the remainder of their lives.'

I didn't pay too much attention to what he said and forgot it soon after.

The film showing was in its last two weeks when a carnival set up in a field near to the chapel. I had used this field with Martin at least once a day before the carnival. I thought twice about it now with the carnival there. Travelling folk are well known for their large and vicious dogs. This seemed to have escaped Father Reilly, who brought his Labrador there as usual, only to have him badly savaged by one of the carnival dogs.

Father Reilly was out of a lot of money in vet fees due to this, and his dog was now afraid to go out. Father Reilly did not know if it would ever recover. I advised him that he should give it time, remembering what had happened to Martin. He said that he would, but it was all too much, his dog was a bag of nerves and eventually he had to have it put to rest. It was a sorry business, all of this, for Father Reilly had been extremely fond of his Labrador.

Not long after the film shows, a young man who had once been a local boy was to be ordained into the priesthood. This was a big thing for Father Reilly. The young man was the first of his many altar boys to go the full distance, to become a priest. Father Reilly asked if I had ever been to an ordination, the first blessing of a new priest. When I told him I hadn't, he said that I should come. 'It is a moving experience, when a man becomes a priest.'

When my mother heard about the ordination, she wanted to come with me. She believed it had a special power. Quite a number of the faithful do, and who was I to say it hadn't?

Here I am Lord, it is I Lord, I have heard you calling in the night.

In the chapel on the day I had never seen so many priests on an altar before. There had to be at least thirty of them, and the Bishop. My mother and I had arrived early, which was just as well. The chapel was so packed that there were people outside, standing in the forecourt. This was before the mass had even begun or the choir assembled. When the mass finally began the priests trooped on to the altar, followed by the Bishop.

The novitiate was twenty-three years old. He was fresh-faced, fair-haired and dressed in a plain white vestment. He was a marked contrast to the thin and old Bishop in *his* vestments: flowing robes and a big, square-shaped hat that was white and gold and a good two foot tall. Soon he was sitting in a huge carved-wood chair. It had all the appearance of a throne. This High Mass was solemn and sombre, more dignified than moving. The young man was giving his life to God of his own choosing. He had direction in his life. How different my life would have been had I found such direction when I was twenty-three years old!

Here I am Lord, it is I Lord, I have heard you calling in the night.

At the close of the mass the novitiate prostrated himself before the Bishop and was ordained. Immediately after, one by one Father Reilly and the other priests embraced the new man in their fold. My own father should have been up there, I thought, on the altar with the priests. That quarry man had been as holy, or holier, as any one of them.

★ * ★

When Martin was six years old he injured his back and could barely walk. At first I thought of a heart attack, it had come on so suddenly. We were just out of a park where, not long before, he had been running like the wind, full of energy. I took pride in Martin's fitness. But on the street he was suddenly all hunched up. He could not lift his head and his spine was ridged and his tail was down and he had a cramped-up, crab-like movement.

'What ails you, Martin?'

He struggled on and we made it home and I began to think that it might not be all that serious, whatever had happened to him. I was further heartened when he wolfed down all his dinner. But later he was nothing like his bouncing self and, when my mother asked what was wrong with him, I said I didn't know.

His head drooped and his body hunched. I was beginning to think it was more of a spinal injury of some kind than a heart attack, for he was making little yelps of pain each time he moved. I would need to take him to a vet to find out what was wrong.

The vet, Mr Wilson, was a beefy guy in a white coat. He had a young female trainee with him in his surgery. He told me to lift Martin up on to a high table, under a bright white light. He felt Martin's body and neck, and his trainee did the same, and he asked her what *she* thought was wrong with him.

'Tell me,' I said.

'We'll need to X-ray Martin,' the vet said.

'What do *you* think it is?'

'Spondylitis.' He went on to explain about a swelling in the spinal cord which was hitting Martin's nerves. 'That's the reason why he cannot raise his head.' He looked me in the eye. 'You might well need to consider putting Martin to sleep, Mr Healy.'

Martin looked like an animal to be put to sleep, all clenched together and his tail between his legs. It would have been inhuman to have taken him home that way and I agreed that Mr Wilson would hold on to him for further examination after the X-ray. I signed a paper to allow for an anaesthetic. Mr Wilson promised to do all that he could, but he said he had no great hopes and that I should prepare for the worst.

'You don't want to see him like this, do you?'

'No, of course I don't.'

'I won't do anything until I see you again.'

Walking home, I felt so fucking lonely. My right-hand man—that was what I sometimes called Martin, and only half in jest—had brought me a new self-worth, changed me from the wretched creature I had been. I did not want a return to that. Neither did my mother.

'Where is Martin?' she asked worriedly when I arrived home.

'With the vet.'

'Is he alive?'

'He was when I last saw him.' I sat in my chair. 'It's his spine,' I said, 'something about spondylitis.'

'What are they going to do for him?'

'They'll stop the pain.'

'To get him better.'

'They're not too sure they can get him better. You saw the pain that he was in.'

'He's strong.'

'He might be strong, but he's not immortal.'

My mother made us two cups of tea.

'God spare Martin,' she said.

'I hope he does.'

'I think he will.'

'We'll see,' I said. 'I've to see the vet again tomorrow.'

It might not be right to care for a dog as much as I cared for Martin. But what is right in this world? For whatever reason, my best pal possessed four legs instead of two. That was all, nothing more. I was not a pitiful man.

The next day I returned to Mr Wilson's surgery, fearing the worst. As soon as he saw me, Mr Wilson said, 'He will need to go on steroids.'

'It was spondylitis?'

'It was and *is*.' Mr Wilson had Martin's X-ray. 'Do you want to see it?'

'No. I couldn't read it.'

'Some dogs pull through, others don't. It is a serious condition.'

'I'll help him all I can.'

'I am sure you will.' Mr Wilson went on to tell me that the steroids could have side-effects, but that Martin had to take them. 'They are the only treatment for his condition.'

I was given an appointment for the following week and told to sit outside in the waiting room to collect my dog. When he was brought out I thought, *my* dog? I would not have recognized Martin had he not known me, so worn and aged had he become. And smaller, without heft. He looked to have lost ten pounds. A stranger, to look at anyhow, and he was on unsteady legs, still woozy from the anaesthetic. My old pal! He was looking it: old. A far cry from the Martin I knew.

When we got home, I took a closer look at Martin. I

noticed a bump on his head, between his ears—it was sharp, like a broken bone—that had not been there before. It soon became apparent that this new Martin was awfully clumsy too. And not just clumsy—blind!

I telephoned Mr Wilson. 'You should have told me that my dog is blind!'

'I didn't know.'

'Well, you know now.'

The vet was silent for a moment. 'What are you going to do?'

'I hoped that you could tell me that. What I can do?'

'Give him a week, his sight might come back.'

'*Might*?'

'It sometimes does,' Mr Wilson said. 'You can never tell what can happen after a general anaesthetic.'

I thought to mention the bump on Martin's head, but his sight was more important.

'This thing gets worse and worse,' I said.

'I told you that it was serious.'

'You didn't tell me he might go blind!'

And Martin was blind, so far as I could tell. But he slept most of the time and it was hard to weigh up his condition. Then, after the best part of a week, he seemed to gain some energy and could suddenly see again. But his tongue was out and he could not get enough to drink, water by the bucketful. Two, three gallons a day at least. The vet told me that this was a side-effect of the steroids I had to give him. I would fancy that steroids had caused his blindness, even if Mr Wilson was not saying. Another side-effect was his balance: he would often fall down, and when we went out to the field I often had to carry him home in my arms. He was slack and loose. The steroids would buck him up again and in turn he would drink more water. This went on for days on end before, little by little, he began to improve, to regain his balance.

When we returned to the vet I complained about the water-drinking. Mr Wilson sympathized, but I had to continue with the steroids. They were all that was holding Martin up. But I could reduce the dosage as time went on, he said, and then stop them altogether.

So Martin was recovering, but not recovered. There was still a problem with his hind legs: the paws were moving in too close together. A fraction more and he would have been all tied up and unable to walk at all. That's what would happen, I was warned, if the steroids were reduced too quickly.

We attended Mr Wilson once a week for the next five weeks. I had to pay for each appointment and it added up

to a considerable sum of money. Mr Wilson did not under-
value himself and his services. I did not begrudge what I
paid him, but I could not keep it up. I was out of work and
now owed money to my sister for Mr Wilson's treatment.

Money had never been a big thing with me. It had come
and gone, mostly gone. But with this new turn for Martin,
and the pricey vet, I determined not to be in a similar way
again. In a few weeks, when Martin was better, if not quite
his old self, I hit on an idea that might support both of us
and founded Doberman Securities. This was my first business venture in more than twenty years and I included
Martin in it. He was the only asset that I had.

I placed a couple of small ads in Glasgow newspapers,
offering our services as security guards. Within days I was
contacted by a Mrs Smart, and we arranged a time for an
interview. Mrs Smart turned out to be an attractive, dark-
haired woman. She was looking for two men and two dogs
to provide night security for an engineering firm which
she was a director of. Would I be interested? I told her that
Doberman Securities consisted of only myself and Martin
and we were just starting up in business.

'What did you do before Doberman Securities?'

I told her that I was a failed writer, but I was still hoping.

Mrs Smart asked if I was a *published* failed writer. I said I was, that I had won two Scottish Arts Council Awards for Literature. This impressed Mrs Smart, and she asked if I intended to write while I did security work. I told her yes, that I intended to continue to write. This seemed to please her too, but she said she required *two* men and *two* dogs.

'Seven nights a week is too much to ask any man to do.'

'I would do it.'

'What about your social life?'

'I don't have much of a social life.'

'Haven't you got a family?'

'No. I've never been married. It is only me and Martin.'

'Martin?'

'My dog.'

'I see.'

'Well, I can't hire you as Doberman Securities,' she said. 'But there is another option.'

There was? Mrs Smart had protruding black eyes that seemed to look right through you.

'You could be employed by us.'

'Employed as *what*?'

'Our chief of night security.'

What a strange encounter. Mrs Smart was going out of her way to help me. Why? I was a total stranger. So was Martin. And yet we were to be her night security. I had no references, nothing. When I enquired the wages, they were more than generous and I arranged to start the following Monday night. Twelve-hour shifts of eight till eight for me and 'Big Boy Peterson'. I had taken to calling Martin Big Boy Peterson after the white heavyweight who had been knocked out by Joe Louis in the 1930s.

Inside the engineering factory I hit a time clock at intervals throughout the night. This was to ensure that I was on the job and not asleep. It was an okay job. I had an office where I could write and Martin did the guarding, what guarding there was to do. Precious little. There were no attempted robberies in the time that I was there. But it employed security as an insurance issue, for the place was full of machinery.

One night, in the early hours, Mrs Smart telephoned to ask how I was getting on. I told her fine and we talked a bit. She asked me to call her Alice. I thought she had a drink in her, that she *had* to have a drink in her.

'Can I call you Thomas?' she said.

'You certainly can, if you want.'

She was flirting with me, Mrs Smart. Alice. I was flattered of course, but wondered why. My mother thought I was not bad-looking and Martin thought I was a not bad guy. So I had two admirers up till now. Was Alice an unlikely third? It would seem to be. She had gotten hold of a book that contained four of my short stories, and such was her high praise that I could have thought to have won the Nobel Prize.

'Do you read much, Alice?'

'I try to do, when I have time. But rarely fiction. I can't remember the last time I read fiction before I read your short stories.'

'Can I ask you why you read my stories?'

'I was curious.'

'I see.' But I didn't see. 'I'm glad you liked them.'

'Have you more short stories for me to read?'

'I have.' She was the first person in a long time to show interest in my writing. 'I would love you to read my other stories, Alice.'

I left them for her at the office in a big brown envelope marked FOR THE ATTENTION OF MRS SMART. When she phoned to thank me, I asked her for a date. I had determined to do so, for I wanted to get to know her. What it was she was about and what did she see in me? We arranged to meet on the following Saturday in a pub in the West End.

The pub was round the corner from the Hillhead subway station. I was a little late and she was already there, sitting with a gin and tonic. This was the first time that I had been alone, without Martin, for many months. The thought had hit me on the subway, how long now we had been pals and how odd it was to be alone, without him.

Alice's eyes looked even darker than I remembered. She wore a loose cardigan and blue jeans. A quizzical smile. She had a gold side tooth. I apologized for being late.

'But you are here,' Alice said. 'I knew you wouldn't let me down.'

Let *her* down!

'It is good to see you again.'

I wondered why she said this. She made me feel good, wanted, something like Martin did. I must be as big a sucker for affection as any man who ever lived. But I was attracted to Alice too. Once I had gotten used to her eyes, I became very attracted. I had been with better-looking women, but she was more exciting. She was older too; in her fifties, I thought. You could tell by her neck and the backs of her hands, which, as a sign of vulnerability, I found most endearing.

'It is good to see *you* again,' I said.

'What are you thinking?'

'That you look different dressed in jeans.'

'Did you think I would be wearing a business suit?'

'I didn't know what to think.'

'Do I surprise you?'

'Very much.'

'I sometimes surprise myself,' she said. 'Do you?'

'What?'

'Surprise yourself.'

'Now and then I surprise myself.' We sat alone in a corner of the pub. 'When I bought Martin I surprised myself.'

'How long have you had Martin?'

'Six years.' I told Alice how I had come to buy Martin. 'I thought I was crazy for a few weeks afterwards.'

'We all do, sometimes. Things we do. I thought I was crazy after phoning you.'

'Why was that?'

'Well, I'm no spring chicken, am I?'

'You look wonderful to me.'

'Are you going to ask me for a rise?'

I said no. Alice changed the subject. She said that she was a widow and had a grown-up daughter.

'Is she married?'

'Not yet.'

I thought to ask how old her daughter was, but we were still at a surface level. This fledgling romance. It was better to let her do the talking. I tend to probe, to ask direct questions. Some people find this off-putting and clam up and I did not want Alice to clam up. We had been getting along too well. Alice's daughter could have been forty for all I cared.

Which was just as well, for her daughter was forty-one. I would learn that later from Alice, who, far from the fifty-three or fifty-four that I had thought, was sixty-three years old.

We dallied a bit, as soon-to-be lovers will, before she asked if I wanted to go home with her. I did and we had a fantastic afternoon together. Alice's breasts were firm, tilted up, she had a pert behind and her belly was taut and rounded. There was nothing to hint at her true age and I thought that I was lucky, such a woman.

After she'd told me her true age, she said, 'Do you still want me?'

'You know I do.'

'I told you I was no spring chicken.'

'I don't care.'

'We could be good for one another.'

'You've been good for me already.'

'I liked you straight away,' she said, 'when you walked into my office.'

'Was that the reason I got the job?'

'What do you think?'

'I think it was.'

'Of course it was.'

'It is usually the other way round, that I should have given *you* a job.'

'You might have done when I was young.'

'You are an attractive woman *now*.'

'I was more attractive *then*.'

'I like you just the way you are.' In bed with Alice, her head on my chest. 'I think that you are beautiful.'

'Most men like younger women.' She had a thing about her age, did Alice.

'You are the goods for me,' I told her. 'I don't give a damn how old you are.'

That night Alice phoned the factory. 'We could hire another man and dog to give you some time off,' she said. 'It would not affect your wage.'

I went with Alice for the next year. She was an excellent, all-round companion. We were equals, and in all that time I did not give thought to the difference in our ages.

I took Alice to the publication party for my first novel and she was so proud, proud of *me*.

'It is not everyone who can write a book.'

The novel earned me 300 pounds, which was less than one week's wages at the factory with Martin.

'But you have proved you can do it.'

I wondered. My novel had about four reviews and sold less than 100 copies. Alice was my only fan, applauder.

I had two nights off each week, which I spent with Alice. She was the reason that I *had* them off and I was not complaining. I could not have wished for a better, more compatible companion, this able woman. She knew what she wanted and went for it, a direct approach. What she had seen in me I do not know. It might have been, to begin at least, that I was a younger man, but not too young to appear to be out of place with her. Forty-eight, the age I was, and sixty-three is not too far out for a man and woman if they get along.

'Have you seen *Swan Lake*?' she asked me one day.

'Is it an opera?'

'It's a ballet.'

'No,' I said. 'I haven't seen it.'

'Would you like to see it?'

'Are you asking me to go with you to see *Swan Lake*?'

'I think that you might like it.'

'We'll see.'

'You don't think you'll like it?'

'No.'

We went and I did—I adored *Swan Lake*. It was the beginning of a passion for me, and the sad thing is I had not discovered it before.

★ * ★

I was in class at school with Jimmy Boyle for three years, from age twelve to fifteen. We were never pals but I remember him vividly. He was a boy with a *presence*. He had gone to St Francis Primary while I was at St Bonaventure's. But we had both failed the 'qualie'—the eleven-plus examination to section off the more intelligent pupils from the dunces. I scored miserable marks and Boyle must have too, for we ended up in the same class, in the worst school, in the worst neighbourhood in the Glasgow of that time.

Boyle's special pal was a boy named Padgy Gallagher. Padgy had brown eyes while Jimmy's were blue. It is the thing I remember most about Boyle, the blueness of his eyes. It was quite startling. At St Bonaventure's Secondary School, Boyle was much like the other boys, feeling his way. I can't remember him to be anything like a stand-out for the first year or so. The school was full of wild guys and it took something extra special—which Boyle would prove to be—to be a stand-out in that place.

Had Boyle gone to a decent school, where the arts were encouraged, his aggression—and he would become very aggressive, explosive—could have been channelled differently. But he was in the right place at the right time to become a gangster. There were a few boys at St Bonaventure's who went on to become gangsters. Not in Boyle's league, but they were tough enough and far too tough for me.

For myself, in such a school of ruffians, I kept a low profile. For a timorous boy, St Bonaventure's was next best to a nightmare. No wonder I wanted out of it, to team up with Billy Bunter and Bob Cherry and the other boys at Greyfriars. I could have enjoyed that school, but any school would have been better than St Bonaventure's. When I think of my time in that school I can become very angry.

I was almost paralysed with fear from the ever-present threat of violence. Those three years had a lasting, bad effect on me. I did not want to know about violence, yet I joined a boxing club. The boxing—watching other people fight, that is—was to become an obsession. It was on two nights a week and Sunday afternoons. I became quite good at skipping rope and punching bags, but I did not like the sparring, no. As Joe Louis said, there is no hiding place in a boxing ring, and the first time I was hit was my last time in a ring. I think I accepted I was a coward after that. In truth, I was more suited to ballet than to boxing when I was fourteen years old. I was to shift from one extreme to yet another throughout my whole life.

Boyle was well on his way to a life of crime when he was fourteen. I think that he had already seen the inside of a remand home by then. He was one fierce boy, no mistake. I would not say I admired him, but there was a certain fascination. Something about the guy. He had a flair for leadership. He was not bad-looking. You heard stories about him. Some of the kids in his class were already in his gang, The Skull. It was a rough bunch, with Boyle in the lead. Who else? He was the most violent boy and violence is the main criterion to lead a gang. The Skull used to fight with other gangs on the streets at night and it soon gained a reputation. Nothing to the reputation that Boyle would have in his later life, but it was a start in the gangs for him.

It is history now, the old Gorbals. St Bonaventure's has long been gone, closed down and then demolished. The name of the place had become too much. Its most famous pupil is now in France, a self-made man.

I read in a newspaper that Jimmy Boyle had settled in the south of France. This was the first in a long time that I had thought of my old classmate of all those years ago. He had been through a lot, and had put other people through a lot. Three murder charges and fifteen years in prison. Not the first time he had been in prison, but it was the longest and the last time that Boyle was in prison. He emerged from it a different man, a sculptor and an author.

In Boyle's book *A Sense of Freedom*, he reflects on his early days in St Bonaventure's. I had read it years before, before I had had Martin, and as a fellow writer I was a trifle jealous. Had it been the usual ghosted hogwash I would have laughed, but this was *real*. The growing-up time at least, for I was there and knew the truth of that. Yet, all the time, my time at school, I thought there was another side to Jimmy Boyle, that there was more to him than met the eye. Of all the boys I knew at school, I would have selected Boyle for the most likely one to have gone to the ballet with me—if, that is, no one else had known.

We did not know about the ballet. And I would not know of that delight until I met with Alice.

* * ★

I learned a lot with Alice. She had a car and would drive us to Edinburgh. There we saw *Swan Lake* and would go on to see *Madame Butterfly,* which I enjoyed almost as much as I had *Swan Lake.* I began to look forward to a new ballet or to an opera with the same excitement as I had once looked forward to a heavyweight title fight. Well, in a way.

Alice was bringing out a new side to my nature. I was more at ease with the theatre crowd than I had ever been with the boxing mob. A clash in cultures, but my life had been full of clashes.

I had been going with Alice for a couple of months when she told me she was Jewish. It did not mean a thing to me and I was surprised to think she thought it might.

'Did you not suspect?' she asked.

'I didn't care.'

'You didn't think.'

'No,' I said. 'I didn't think.' And that was that. But it hung in my head, that she had thought her being Jewish was so important.

I had a really great time with Alice. Some click, connection. She wanted me and I wanted her. We enjoyed our nights in Edinburgh. There was no unease, if, in many

ways, we were complete opposites. She was posh and edu-
cated, a hint of glamour, of the woman she had once been.
A way she looked, the throw of her head. It made me feel
old when she looked like that, even for only a moment. But
you can't hold time and there were other moments when
she looked all her years. This did not bother me. Far better, as I saw it, to have a once-beautiful older woman than
a twenty-year-old plain Jane.

Alice had been a widow for five years when I first met
her and I was, so she said, her first male companion in that
time.

We had the usual and not so usual disagreements. We
had been together for all of a year when Alice suggested a
holiday. She wanted to go abroad together, but I told her I
could not do that, because of Martin. I was deserting him
too much already to be with her. I was now off work three
nights a week and almost *living* with her. This had had a
distressing effect on Martin, who had long been with me
night and day. I could not, not even for a holiday with
Alice, leave him for two weeks.

'Are you telling me you have not been on holiday since
you got Martin?' she asked.

'Only to caravans.'

'Do you mean *with* Martin, you went to caravans?'

'I do. He was the reason I went to caravans, that we could be together.'

Alice thought this was a bit much, that I would not leave Martin to go on holiday. 'You can't let a dog rule your life.'

I thought that I couldn't let her either.

'Most people put their dogs in kennels,' she said.

'I'm not most people.'

'Do you prefer to be with him than to be with me?'

'I've known him longer than I've known you.'

'You would do without a holiday with me to be with him?'

'You could holiday with *us.*'

'In a caravan?'

'I can't leave Martin for two weeks.'

'You mean that you don't *want* to leave Martin for two weeks.'

'If you want to put it that way.'

'I can't see any other way *to* put it.'

'You could come with us to a caravan.'

It ended up that she went alone while I stayed at home with Martin. Was I making her feel, in her mind, second to a dog? This had to rattle. She had paid for our nights at the theatre, and she had wanted to pay for our holiday too, to be with me. But I—it seemed to Alice—had preferred to be with Martin. I would have liked to have gone with Alice, but I would have been rotten company, worrying about my dog. It was our first real quarrel; there was no give or take.

There was a certain cooling afterwards, when she returned from holiday. No 'wish you had been there' or things like that. We did not speak about where she'd been and what she'd seen, the people she had met. She had been hurt and was not about to hide it. We did not meet for a good two weeks after she had come home. I had phoned of course, but she had put me off—she had this to do and that—and I began to think that she might have met another man on holiday when, late at night, she telephoned the factory and we arranged to meet.

Martin was much happier when it had been just me and him again. The way that it had always been, until Alice. I swear that he knew it when she phoned. Some *sense*. They were beginning to be rivals, bitter foes.

'How is Martin?' she asked.

'Just dandy.'

'That's good.'

Some hope.

'How are you?'

Alice paused. 'I'm missing you.'

'You don't *need* to miss me.'

'I'm only second best to you.'

'Please don't start all that again.'

'I can't help it.'

And neither she could, as I found out. A bickering Alice. This might sound crazy, but it was all too true. Really, we should have finished it then; given that she felt a *wronged* woman, it had to finish soon anyhow.

'I've had Martin since he was six weeks old!'

'That's not the point.'

'It is with me.'

'Did you tell *him* you loved him?'

'Don't be daft.'

'It could be the other way round,' she said. 'Who's the daft one here?'

'What do you mean?'

'I think you know.'

She now felt fit to threaten me. I told her to fuck off.

Within the week I got the sack. It was not a surprise. In truth I had been waiting for it and the only surprise was that it had taken her so long, to be rid of me completely. I was out of her life as quickly as I had come into it. She would have had me out of house and home, if she could have done; myself and Martin. Two vagabonds. As it was I only lost my job. I had saved some money and it was no disaster. But Alice's revenge was hard to credit. All because of how I felt for Martin.

★ * ★

In June of 1991 the American evangelist Billy Graham came to preach at Celtic Park in Glasgow. My sister had come by two tickets for this event and she asked if I would go with her. I was not too keen on Billy Graham. The man was a Baptist, a Protestant, and I was of course of the Church of Rome. When I explained this to my sister I was told that I was a bigot. 'You want to have an open mind. What harm can he do to you?'

I suspected none, and to prove I was no bigot I agreed to accompany her. She had booked seats on a church bus that would take us to Celtic Park. A gathering of Christians. It was a humid, grey-skied early evening. Billy Graham had been preaching at Celtic Park for a week and this was the last night of his current crusade.

Celtic Park is famous for its football side, Glasgow Celtic. The club was founded by Irish Catholics and it flies the tricoloured flag of the Republic of Ireland. Most of its supporters are of Irish descent, and there is a huge rivalry between them and the supporters of Glasgow Rangers, who are true-blue Protestants. The Celtic supporters are pro-IRA, and, outside of Belfast, Glasgow is the most bigoted city in the world, Catholic against Protestant. The shame of the city, and it is a shame in its truest sense. This religious bigotry often leads to trouble when the two sides meet, and I can't say that the Catholic Church has tried to ease the situation. You get Catholic priests who are every bit as bigoted as the followers of Celtic. It would not be the first time that a priest has interrupted his service to announce from the altar that Celtic had scored a goal. I consider this an abomination and I have walked out of a chapel because of it. I do not go to chapel to listen to football scores. There are some priests I can't abide for all their so-called calling.

Billy Graham must have known all this. He must also have known that Celtic Park is something of a sacred shrine to Glasgow's Catholic population. But this was the place where he chose to speak, to spread his message, to give Glasgow *hope.* On the church bus, there was a festival air from the very start. When we arrived at Celtic Park the place was full of buses. There were a number of policemen, but more I think for traffic duty than for any anticipation of trouble. Outside of the stadium there was a lot of Billy Graham memorabilia for sale. One of the most popular was a red rosette with the words WE VE BEEN TO SEE BILLY GRAHAM in white.

Inside the park I was surprised by the attendance. There had to be 20,000 people, and, unlike in the Roman Catholic Church, where it is mostly oldies who attend, a lot of them were in their teens and twenties. It made for a change, if nothing else. I was warming to the atmosphere, a feeling of Christian values in spite of the different religious denominations. Jesus had died on the cross for all of us. For some reason, perhaps my upbringing, that truth had escaped me until that night at Celtic Park. Or had I been a bigot? I don't know. I would always be a Catholic, because I believed in Catholicism; but there is only one God for all Christians.

My sister and I sat above the choir and there was a red carpet that stretched out over the pitch to a podium where Billy Graham stood. He was a large, solid-looking man and was dressed in a grey suit. He had a mass of white hair and a ruddy, high complexion. He was in his seventies, and— you would have thought—long past his best. Not that night. I have never been so enthralled. The man had a gift that was almost genius. Standing on the podium speaking about Sodom, he *took* you there, to Sodom. A frightful place, where, outwith Lot, there was not one other righteous man. I had heard the story before, but how had a man such as Lot—who was good and pure and spoke to God—come to be in such a place? Billy Graham soon explained. He told the story first hand, as though *he* was Lot, and you could hear the anger in his voice. It was not at all theatrical. This was a man who truly believed and, with little more persuasion, could have had me believing too. A wrathful God. I felt sorry for Lot when, before his eyes, his wife had turned into a pillar of salt. This, and I thought it harsh, was her punishment for looking back on the erupting Sodom—it was destroyed by fire and brimstone—when she had been warned not to do so. It was easily the best sermon I had ever heard.

On the church bus going back, my sister asked what I thought of the night and Billy Graham. The sheer sincerity of the man had had a huge effect on me.

'I thought that it was brilliant.'

'Poor Lot's wife.'

'Poor Lot,' I said. 'It could have been no joke for him when his wife became a pillar of salt.'

'You don't believe it, do you?'

I was about to say that stranger things had happened, but *had* they? A pillar of salt.

'I don't think so.'

'You don't *think* so?'

'It was along time ago, who knows what happened?'

My sister looked at me like I was mad. 'You are to take the Old Testament with a pinch of salt.'

'Billy Graham doesn't.'

'No,' she said. 'It's more a *block* of salt for him.'

'He's an old-style sort of preacher.' It had begun to rain outside, to really hammer down, and you could hear it drum on the roof of the bus. 'Who is to say he is right or wrong?'

The rain continued, an almost biblical deluge, after we had left the bus with our fellow Christians. I now thought of myself more of a Christian, with a leaning to Catholicism. A taxi took us home through the streets of a flooded Glasgow. My sister cracked a joke about Noah's Ark.

Martin and me were back to the fields and long, long walks. I had published a second novel and had gained a Writer's Bursary from the Scottish Arts Council. This was the first for many years, since the time I had bought Martin, that I had money to spare. I was beginning to think that my luck had changed when, right out of the blue in March of 1992, my mother came down with a stroke. A bad one.

She was eighty-two and had never known a day's ill-health. After the stroke, she would not know a day's good health. The doctor said that he was sorry, but that she was old and I had been lucky to have had her for so long. I told him that the longer you have somebody the more you want to keep them. He understood, or so he said, but said there was nothing could be done for her. I was told that she would end her days in hospital.

My poor mother. She hardly knew just where she was or what was happening to her. What *had* happened to her on a blink. She had gone out of the house to a shopping van to collect some groceries. Suddenly, she fell backwards and collapsed. She was carried back inside the house, all twisted up and paralysed down her left side. I had just left the house with Martin, and someone chased and caught up with me and I was told I must go home. I remember looking at her left hand. It was tightly clenched, like in a fist, and it would stay that way until she died, some two years later. That fucking stroke! She was unlucky to have survived it. Far better for her, and for my sister and me, had it killed her. This in retrospect, for at the time I still had hope she might recover, come back to something like herself, the mother she had been.

Three months before we had gone to our usual Midnight Mass, and she had been slower then, but there had been no indication of what was to come. I had kidded with her as usual, about pious frauds and fraudulent pass-keepers, and she had to laugh as usual. My mother could never keep a straight face for very long when I was with her inside the chapel. It was all crazy stuff, but it amused us both. Alas, we would be amused no more. That was the final mass for us together—and for me. I have never been back to a Midnight Mass again.

She was slouched on a sofa and could move only her right arm. Martin would not go near to her, knowing that something was wrong. *Something?* Nothing was right and she was deathly white and I thought that she might die. What to do? I went for the priest, Father Reilly. The Last Rites: I thought it the proper thing to do, at the time, but I do not think it now. No. The Last Rites are meant for solace, but from what I saw of that frightful ceremony, I would not recommend it for anyone still conscious.

My mother was frightened enough without the sudden arrival of the priest to make her even more so. He had wasted no time, I will say that for Father Reilly. When, panting and out of breath, I had knocked on the door of the chapel house, he drove us back to our house immediately. I had to lock Martin away for the time that he was there. Not long, but time enough to scare my mother even more. For all that she might have been befuddled, she was only too aware of that priest and what was going on.

After Father Reilly left, my mother asked if I would help her to the toilet. I tried, of course, but it was hopeless. She was all at odds and so was I. I have never felt so awkward and helpless as I did then.

I sat in a chair across from her and we spoke a bit and she told me that at the instant of the stroke she had felt to have been risen up and that she could *see* the rooftops. I told her that she was down again and would get better. I was not to know it at the time, but this was to be the last logical conversation that I would have with my mother.

When the doctor arrived he phoned in an ambulance. It was about all that he could do. My sister had come home from her work by then and she went to the hospital with our mother. This terrible day! The worst in all my life. I sat in the house alone with Martin. He was very subdued and seemed to sense the enormity for both of us of what had happened.

At this time I was attending a Tuesday night novena in St Francis Chapel in the Gorbals. The novena was in honour of St Anthony, who, so it is said, once held the child Jesus. I walked down there with Martin and we sat at the back of the chapel. St Francis Chapel is gone now, but for 100 years or more it was an institution in the Gorbals.

You were to complete nine consecutive Tuesdays for a complete novena. I was only one away when my mother took a stroke. It is said that the closer you get to nine the harder it is to make it. I don't know the truth of that, but Martin—for he was making the novena too—and I were stopped at eight.

On the ninth Tuesday, I was visiting in Ward 10 in the Victoria Hospital rather than at St Anthony's novena. My mother was there for two weeks for assessment. It was outside this ward that I was told that she would end her days in hospital. What did *he* care, that doctor? It is a trouble for older patients that they are often regarded as nuisance value, wasting space.

This was my first first-hand experience of serious illness. My mother had been so sweet and gentle, and she had a fragility in her old age that I had found endearing. I had thought that she would potter on until she was a hundred. But it was not to be. The stroke had seen to that. She had been rendered incontinent and paralysed. Half of the cells in her brain were dead.

In the general upset of this time Martin had to be left to himself a lot. This was the first time in all the years I'd had him that he was without my company, and I hope that he felt not too neglected.

One morning I received a phone call from the hospital informing me that my mother was being moved from the Victoria to the Samaritan, which was something of a staging post for patients such as her, who were in for life, until they died. The Samaritan is now a block of flats, but then it was near to a place named Eglinton Toll. I must have passed it many times and yet I did not know of its existence. I wish I had never known of its existence.

The Samaritan had a small yard and on good days I would sit there with my mother for a breath of air. She was in a wheelchair by then. I hated that I had to *wheel* her, and so did she. My mother, for all she was old, had been fiercely independent. For my part, I had to wonder what it was all about that she had lived until eighty-two to suddenly come to this.

'How is wee Martin?'

'He's fine.'

'I miss wee Martin.'

'I can bring him here to visit you.'

'That would be good. I'd love to see wee Martin again.'

But when I brought Martin to see her she did not know him. You could just never tell with my mother now, for she would say one thing one minute and change her mind the next. Then she was forgetful and, the day after, or it might have been one hour after, she could not remember Martin's visit. This stroke business, you never knew just where you were. Still my mother had appeared to be getting a little better, more lucid and aware of her surroundings inside the Samaritan, when I was told that she was to be transferred again.

Soon she was sent to a geriatric unit, one which, so far as old folk are concerned, is about the end of the line in Glasgow. It was a nightmare place. Half of the patients were bruised from falls, and bandaged heads were common. I could not at first believe the number of sore faces. This boxing ring of a hospital—if you could call it that, a hospital. Where had all the nurses gone? There were damn few that I could see in this place of wizened, battered faces. After some months there, I took her home. This was against all medical advice, but I had to do it. Something in me. She had been declining, no question; and I hoped that she might improve at home, familiar surroundings and all. My sister and me and Martin. Once again, she was asking about Martin.

'How is the wee dog?'

'He is doing fine, but missing you.'

It had been in my head that we might go round to the Midnight Mass the following month, December. When I took my mother out of hospital she was dressed in the same clothes as when she had first gone in, nine months before.

We had come home by ambulance. My mother had been sitting in the hospital in a wheelchair waiting for me. I remember that she smiled and I thought she looked mischievous, as she might have looked when she was a little girl.

'We are going home.'

'Thanks be to God.'

And home we went. The house had been prepared for her, a commode and a special chair and a hospital bed. Nurses were to visit three times each day. I had high hopes for success with this and a better sort of life for my mother. But I had not bargained for the mental side, the personality changes that a stroke can bring. From a quiet, mild-mannered sort of person my mother had become loud and quite demanding. I had noticed this change in hospital, but had chosen to think it was the hospital that had caused it, the almost nonexistent nurses. I began to learn otherwise in a very short time indeed. Inside the house and out, in the chapel. I took her around to a twelve o'clock Sunday mass. We sat at the back, behind the pews. The chapel was half empty and I had been glad of that. My cursing, brawling mother! I had not thought that she had known such language. When people turned to look at her she put out her tongue at them. Had I not been there I wouldn't have believed it. My gentle, caring mother. She frightened a child, who began to scream. The whole chapel was now turned around, looking at us and I had to wheel her out, she was causing such a disturbance.

For all of that it was still good to have my mother home. Whatever else, she was a *presence* in her special chair. Martin stayed away from it and from her. This was not the woman he had known, with her tin of Pal for Christmas. The nurses came and went. My sister was out at work, exhausted. She was often up half of the night attending to our mother. We both loved her very much and were giving it all we had, in a house that had been turned into something like a hospital. The first nurses came at nine o'clock, when—after I had let them in—I would go out for a walk with Martin. My mother would be washed and dressed and in her chair when we returned to give her breakfast. The chair had a sort of table and I would spoon-feed her a cereal. It took for ever and the stuff all running down her face, and I could have cried when I wiped her clean, that we had come to this.

It could not last indefinitely. My mother was in a much worse way than I had thought when I had visited her in hospital. No wonder they had tried to stop me bringing her back home. Had I been outside looking in, I would have tried to stop me from bringing her back home. But I do not regret it, what I did; and I lasted longer doing it than anyone had thought I would. For I did not want to let her go. She retained endearing qualities to me. Her hands. I used to try and open out the fingers of the bad one. I don't know why, but I would think simply to touch her, for her hand was gone, completely dead.

Martin was now nearly nine and he too was causing me concern. His hind legs had a stilted look, as without fluidity. His big paws were becoming awfully slow now. He had always been so quick and nimble, so beautifully balanced.

For a time, some years, there had been no other dog could touch him. My Martin. Had I, in all the trauma of my mother's stroke, failed to notice his decline? I think I had chosen not to notice; but it could not go unnoticed now. Martin was falling apart, and at his age there was nothing any vet could do for him.

My mother, now Martin. This house of pain and suffering, of looming death. It was touch and go between them, for who would go first. And I was none too bright myself. The nursing had gone on now for eleven months and I was worn out with it. The mornings had become an agony, my too-old dog and a too-old me. I was not far off of fifty now and not the man I had been just eleven months before, when my mother had first come home. I had had such high hopes! Old times again. It had been anything but.

Can old times *ever* be the same again? Still, we had tried, my sister and me, and if we were finally beaten it was not for the lack of love and effort.

On my doctor's advice in regard to my own health, I agreed to a respite. Two weeks. He then arranged for my mother to return to the Geriatric Unit. There was no other place would have her. She was chronically ill and nursing homes, as I found out, are only for the aged and feeble.

When the ambulance men came for her I felt a criminal. I almost turned them back again, empty-handed. She looked so small and vulnerable, still in that wheelchair. I had gone to the hospital to take her out, but I could not return to the hospital to put her in again. A grim day. I had tried to explain to my mother that it was only for two weeks, but she did not understand. I kissed her cheek and wheeled her out, into the waiting ambulance.

Martin's hind legs had gone and he had a vacant look at the eyes—they had always been so sharp and bright—and he was messing all over the place. This should not have been allowed to happen, my old pal. Batman and Robin. He had been as proud as punch with me back then. So long ago. In Bude in Cornwall. As Big Boy Peterson. It was the hardest thing to let him go. But I had no option, I knew what I would need to do.

I had, I think, if I did not want to admit to it, put my mother back into hospital to give me time and a hoped-for strength to do the decent thing by Martin. How he was, it could not go on. He was all but crippled now and it was a cruel thing to keep him. And yet I could not let him go. This was the one time in all our years together that I let him down, because I could not bear to part with him. He was old and done. Fucking *time*! It will take everything from you.

The two weeks respite went to three. My sister had left the house to stay with a friend and it was only me and Martin. I would take him out, but it was hopeless, for there was nothing in his legs. He would soon cave in and I would hear his big chest bump the ground. When it came to it, what I should do I couldn't, not for the longest time. I thought that I could face up to anything, but I was not the man I thought.

During my last days with Martin, I saw my mother daily in the Geriatric. It was a shock to me to discover that she could not remember one single day in all the eleven months she had been home. In her head she had always been just where she was, on the moment, since the stroke. This, that she could not remember a single day, one moment to the next, had let me out of my promise to have brought her home within two weeks.

Martin, my dear friend, had never been a dog to me, but he would need to die as one. There was no other way. I had no gun nor, had I one, the heart to shoot him. A *holy* dog? He had made many a novena with me. To St Anthony in the Gorbals. The good times. But for every good there is a bad, in time. And this was the worst time for me if not for Martin. *He* did not know what was going on, this closing of the book.

I telephoned our old vet, Mr Wilson, and arranged a time to take Martin to the surgery. Now, after all my dread, my silly dilly-dallying, it had hit the point where I would be glad to have it over with. The ailing Martin had come to me as a helpless puppy and he was leaving me equally helpless, old and lame. I had to carry him out to a waiting taxi. It was about four o'clock on a November night and I could not speak to Martin, as throughout the years I al-ways had when I was upset. Not this time. He lay at my feet and I could hardly even look at him, knowing, as I did, that in a very short time he would be no more.

Mr Wilson was waiting for us. I had paid outside, at his reception. He bent down and jagged one of Martin's front paws. Seconds after, four at most, Martin fell down on his chest and I dropped his lead and walked out, into the night. I was a man alone, and I *was* alone that night, you bet.

When I met my sister at the hospital I was going to tell her about Martin, but found out I could not. It had always been just me and him; even now when he was dead, it was just me and him. I think I waited a couple of weeks before I told my sister.

'It was the hardest thing I had ever done.'

'You should have told me sooner.'

'I couldn't.'

'I was fond of Martin too.'

But not nearly as fond as I had been and it had not been her who had taken Martin to the vet. The bump of his chest against the floor when he had fallen down. It woke me nights, the bump of his chest against the floor. I could imagine the shock to his heart, the barbiturate overdose.

'You might have been fond of him, but he was my dog.'

'I know he was.'

'I miss him badly.'

'I'm sure you do, but you can get another dog.'

'If I wanted another dog.'

'I have heard that it is the best thing to do, to get another dog when the old one dies.'

Well, it might have been for another man who had another dog, but it was not for me. No way. There would be no two dogs in my life. Having Martin put to sleep had almost killed me, and I could not chance to go through all that again. That and I lacked the patience now to make a big thing of a dog. The trick with Martin was the timing. I had been ready for a dog back then, and I had needed Martin as much as Martin had needed me. I think he saved my life, the way I had been going. A chance read through the *Glasgow Herald,* the livestock column: pups for sale. My taxi ride to see them, to first encounter Martin. The brutal man I had bought him from. I had never seen him again. No matter. The wonderful night at Celtic Park when I had witnessed Billy Graham. I would not have been at Celtic Park if I had not had Martin.

Now, without him, I was on my own again. Flung back on myself, and with my mother back in hospital I had a new freedom. Or so I thought. It was not long before I began to drink again, and once again I ended up in trouble. A couple of fights. I lost two teeth and had a night in jail after one of them. It was all the old, before-Martin behaviour; with one very important difference. I was ten, eleven years older and what I had been before I was not now. In the other fight I had three ribs cracked and almost lost an eye. That had been late at night, but I was back drinking next morning. I would doubt that I drew a sober breath for the best part of three weeks, this crazy drunk. I would have gone on drinking had I not been beaten half to death by two young guys who, for whatever reason—some ancient slight?—had been paid to do me over. I was sick of it all, sick of myself. I did not even try to find out who had hired them.

In the event, I had to go to hospital. I was ambulanced up off the street and stretchered into hospital. There was nothing broken but I was badly bruised and I had internal bleeding. They kept me in hospital for six days. This was long enough to get me sober, to bring me to my senses. In a hospital bed in paper pyjamas. Martin, had he been in the world, would not have wanted *this* for me.

I said a prayer for him, that wherever he was, wherever dogs go—for they must go some place—he was happy there.

I emerged from hospital a stronger, more spiritual man than I had been when I had entered it. I had an acceptance of Martin's passing, which I could not accept before. I determined to pull myself together, to return to the man I had been with him.

When I resumed my visits to my mother, I had a bruise on my forehead. My mother had not missed my visits, but she asked me how I had come by the bruise.

'Martin hit me with his paw.'

'Why did he do that?'

'We were playing.'

She was in a room with three other patients, all of whom were bedridden and in a critical condition. My mother seemed not to notice nor to care about her surroundings, but at least she was out of bed and sitting in her chair.

'You know how I play with Martin.'

'How's he, wee Martin?'

'He's okay.'

'I hope that he's okay.'

'Don't worry about him.'

'I'm worried about *you*.'

Those were the last words that my mother ever spoke to me, for some time during that same night she had a further stroke and the following day she could not speak. This did not seem to alarm her and I wondered then and I wonder still if, given the damage to her brain which had destroyed her memory, she was aware that her voice had gone.

She was disconnecting bit by bit, as a puppet with missing strings. For all of that, she appeared much calmer, more self-contained, and I was glad of that and proud of her. Blood of my blood. In her chair she would try to write with her good hand, so I spoke and she listened, or at least she pretended to. I have no idea. But I do know that she knew me. Since the second stroke I had had the constant dread that one day she might not know me, but I was spared that. She knew me until the end.

I was seldom away from the Geriatric after I had sobered up. My sister was usually there, but rather than bringing us closer, as comrades in this misery, we could only fight and argue. She was still out of the house, staying with her friend, and, given my past behaviour, I suppose that she had every right to fight and argue with me.

I had discovered a small hotel quite near to the hospital where I sometimes went to have a meal, usually fish and chips. This saved me cooking for myself, and as I did not want to be alone in an empty house, it served a double purpose. It was now near to Christmas and I was still missing Martin and I was reminded of the Christmases when I had gone to Midnight Mass and how happy I had been then. My whole world was now collapsing, falling in. I was not long out of hospital and I was fighting to survive, to regain some self-respect.

I had found self-respect with Martin, but it was not right that a man should need a dog as much as I had needed him. Some weakness in my character or something strange in me, in my make-up. There are few men who would settle for a dog in this life. I should have had a wife, children, grandchildren by now. A normal life. It is the way of things. But I had shunned the way of things. I had preferred to go my own way, however bizarre that might have been. There was a lot I had to think about—myself to know—to discover what I was about.

I was something like that, gloomy and introspective, when I met a woman I had seen before—she was a visitor to the Geriatric—in the hotel one night. She was slim and dark and I fancied her in a vague way, which was about all I could fancy anyone at that time. I had made no approaches to her, and, in the hotel, it was her who came to me. Her name was Paula and we had the Geriatric thing in common. She appeared to be as glad of my company as I was of hers. Someone to talk things over with. Adversity can do that, bring people closer. Paula's father, referred to by the staff as the Jewish gentleman, was suffering from senility. I had seen him wandering in the wards dressed in his pyjamas, as though he was looking over the other patients to see how they were getting on. He had been a doctor, so that figured. Paula was also a doctor, a practising psychiatrist. Had I known this initially, when we first spoke, I might have been on my guard with her, to watch what I was saying. For I have always been wary of psychiatrists. Some of them seem harmless, until you learn of their reports, what they have written up on you. Needless to say, I never received a good one. Rather the opposite. But from an innocent start, for I did not know of her profession, I was to get on well with Paula.

I had already eaten, and we sipped coffee. Paula had only come in for coffee. She was worried about her father, who, it seemed, had contracted a virus and was now confined to bed. 'I'm used to him up and about,' she said.

I told her that I too was used to seeing her father doing his rounds, checking on the welfare of his patients.

'He was a doctor for sixty years,' she said.

'It shows.'

'He thinks he is still a doctor.'

'Well, he is in a way, isn't he?'

We had introduced ourselves.

'What do you do, Thomas?'

'I am unemployed.'

'Do you have a profession?'

'Not really, but I have written a couple of books.'

'Then you are a writer.'

'I suppose I am.'

'I would like to read your books.'

'If you meet me here tomorrow night I will give them to you.'

Paula laughed. 'I asked for that, didn't I?'

'Will you meet me here tomorrow night?'

'You don't waste time, do you?'

'Are you married?'

'Would it matter?'

'No, I don't think it would.'

'I am divorced.'

'Then I don't need to worry.'

'Are *you* married?'

I told her no, that I was a bachelor.

'There are not too many of *them* around.'

'I have yet to meet the right woman.'

'Do you think you ever will?'

'I've waited for long enough.'

Paula smiled. At least the conversation had taken a turn away from the Geriatric Unit. 'It's mostly a matter of luck,' she said, 'to be in the right place at the right time. But even then it sometimes—I think most times—does not work out the way you might have hoped it would.'

'It didn't for you?'

'Not towards the end.'

'Were you married for a long time?'

'More than twenty years.' Paula looked at me. 'I might be older than you think I am.'

'But you do know I am attracted to you.'

'I surmised you might be, after you had asked me for a date.'

My chance encounter in the night, in the hotel with Paula. She was a complete stranger, yet it had been on the tip of my tongue to ask if I could spend the night with her. This *had* to be the loneliest that I had ever been. Fearing the night, and the nights are long in Glasgow in December, I wanted someone to hold.

The following night my mother was much the same. I am almost sure that the hospital staff put her in her chair because they knew she would have visitors, my sister and myself. In that hospital at that time a patient who had visitors was better treated than a patient who had none.

Paula's father was still in bed. I made a point of looking into the room where he was being nursed. He appeared to be unconscious, which is not a good sign in any hospital, but it is a particularly bad one in a geriatric unit.

Waiting for Paula in the hotel, she was behind time and I began to think she was not coming, that she had been delayed too long in the hospital or had changed her mind about meeting me. Had I come on too quickly? You can never tell, or I can't; not where women are concerned. I sat back from the bar and sipped a coffee. I had my two books in a plastic bag, to give to Paula when she came. But that was beginning to look like an outside chance.

She was some thirty minutes late, at least, and I was ready to go, when to the leap of my heart—and it leapt all right, I had been so down till then—she suddenly appeared.

'You waited for me.'

'Of course, I waited.'

'I wondered if you would.'

'You must have *known* that I would wait for you.'

'I thought you might, but I could hardly have blamed you if you hadn't.' Paula told me about her hospital visit and how she had to summon a nurse to find out what was going on, the state that her father was in. 'God, I am sick of hospitals. I work in one, you know.'

'Not until now, I didn't.'

'Well, I do. I am a doctor in a hospital for people with mental health problems.'

'That must be interesting.'

Paula rolled up her eyes in a gesture of exasperation. 'People say that all the time, but it is only a job and you get used to head-bangers.'

'Better you than me,' I said. 'I mean, you know what you are doing.'

'Do you think I know what I am doing?'

'I said so, didn't I?'

'But you are only trying to flatter me, to get inside my knickers.' Paula looked me full in the face. 'Tell me I am wrong.'

'I think you might be a little distraught.'

'Distraught my arse,' Paula said, but she could not help smiling. 'No way I am distraught.'

'I'm glad to hear it.'

'You are a funny guy, aren't you?'

'How do you mean funny?'

'You come on like all old-fashioned, a courtly sort.'

'I try to be courteous, if I can.'

'I know you do, but it's all a front.'

'You're the doctor.'

'I would not like to analyse what is inside your head.'

'You have done not badly without trying.'

'Have you brought your writing with you?'

'Sure,' I said. 'I want to try to impress so that I *can* get inside your knickers. Do you think I will?'

'Hang around and you'll find out.' Paula was looking at the covers of my novels. 'You grew up in the Gorbals and left school when you were fifteen,' she said.

'I did.'

'How did you learn to write?'

'I read a lot of books.'

'You just picked it up?'

'More or less.'

'I'm impressed.'

'Wait until you read the books.'

'I'm looking forward to reading them.'

I had bought Paula a coffee, which she'd finished.

'Do you want a drink, or something to eat?'

'Another coffee will do.' She looked at me. 'Don't *you* drink?'

'No, not now. I gave it up.'

'Why did you give it up?'

Most people asked *when*.

'It was getting me into trouble.'

Paula shifted the subject. 'Are you working on something now, another book?'

'No. I wish I was, but I'm not.'

'You were close to your mother, weren't you?'

'I was. I still am. I hate to see her the way she is.'

'I hate to see my father the way he is.'

'I bet he was a good doctor.'

'He was a good man.'

'Do you have children, Paula?'

'One son. But he's married now and has children of his own.'

'That makes you a granny.'

'Does it matter to you that I am a granny?'

'It does not.'

'Have you ever been with a granny before?'

'I don't know. I suppose that I might have been. There are some young grannies these days.'

'But they did not let on that they were grannies.'

'No,' I said.

Paula was dressed like a cowboy girl, in a blue denim jacket and a blue denim skirt and there was nothing grannyish about her.

'I have never had a woman who confessed to me that she was a granny.'

'Except for me.'

'Except for you, but I've not *had* you, have I?'

'I know how old you are. It's on the backs of your books, the year that you were born. I would have taken you for older.'

'I sometimes feel a whole lot older.'

'Since your mother's stroke, do you mean?'

'I do,' I said. 'It all seems now like another world since my mother first took a stroke.'

'Poor Thomas.' Paula put her hand on my knee. 'I think you were much closer to your mother than I was to my father.'

'I used to have a dog too,' I said. 'He was a Doberman named Martin.'

'Do you want to speak about him?'

'I'm not your patient.'

'I don't think of you as a patient.' Paula sort of rubbed my knee. 'You must know that.'

'He was my best pal.'

'Was he your *only* pal?'

'I had acquaintances.'

'But you preferred to be with Martin?'

'After I came to know him I did. We were together most of the time, and he slept on a sofa beside my bed. When you sleep in a room with a dog you soon begin to know that dog.'

'How long did you have Martin?'

'Ten years.'

'That's a long time. Can I ask when he died?'

'Last month, November,' I said. 'I had to take him to the vet and have him put to sleep.'

Paula's hand was still rubbing my knee and upwards, towards my thigh.

'The vet jagged his front paw and Martin fell down and bumped his chest on the floor and then he rolled over on to his side, his paws stretched out in front of him.'

'I used to have a corgi,' Paula said, 'when Reuben— that is my son's name—was a boy.'

'What was the corgi's name?'

'Whistle.'

'Did he come to you when you whistled?'

'He went to Reuben when Reuben whistled.'

'What became of Whistle?'

'He was knocked down and killed instantly when Reuben was out with him.'

'How did Reuben cope with that?'

'He wanted us, his father and me, to buy him another dog.'

'You didn't?'

'No. Whistle had been enough to contend with. He was a lovable little thing, but *so* destructive.'

'Then he must have been young.'

'He was only two when he died.'

'How old is Reuben now?'

'I am not telling you how old he is.'

'What does he do, work at?'

'He is a doctor.'

'I should have guessed. Was his father a doctor too?'

'He was. A heart surgeon.'

'Is he still a heart surgeon?'

'No, he's too old now to be a heart surgeon.'

'You must have had a lot of boyfriends before you married him.'

'I've had a lot of boyfriends *since* I married him,' Paula said. 'He is fifteen years older than I am.'

'Do you have one now?'

'No, not now.'

'When did you last have a boyfriend?'

'Before I became a granny.'

'That's no answer.'

'I've not had a boyfriend for almost six years.'

'You couldn't have been looking.'

'I might have lost interest after I became a granny.'

'Please don't mention *granny* again.'

'When did you last have a girlfriend, Thomas?'

'A couple of years back. Her name was Alice.'

'Were you fond of her?'

'I was,' I said, 'but she was a bit of a bully.'

'How do you mean, a bit of a bully?'

'I was employed by her and I think that she began to think that she owned me.'

'So you got rid of her?'

'No, she got rid of me. It's a strange story, but she was jealous of my dog.'

'Were you more fond of your dog than you were of her?'

'I must have been. I couldn't go on holiday with her because I would have worried about Martin, and she resented that.'

'You don't like being bossed?'

'Who does?'

'Not you, that's evident.'

'We were sacked.'

'I'm sorry to hear that.'

Paula had a withered look, at the eyes. But she had long black hair and thick eyebrows, long lashes. Her mouth was small but she had full red lips.

'Was Alice married, divorced or what?'

'She was a widow.'

'She was older than you?'

'A bit, she was in her sixties.'

'That's more than a bit, if you were only forty-seven. Do you like older women?'

'Not especially. I wasn't looking for an older woman, if that is what you mean.' I put my hand on top of Paula's, on my thigh. 'She just happened along, that was all.'

'Was she *good* to you?'

'She was,' I said, 'but she didn't buy me jewellery or anything like that.'

'You weren't a gigolo, were you?'

'No, I wasn't a gigolo.'

'You just went for the ride?'

I smiled. 'You could say that I was just there for the ride.'

I had never wanted a woman as much as I wanted Paula that night. My first Christmas alone, without Martin, for almost a decade. I missed that dog incredibly, a dull but insistent ache. I knew not what to do without him, as through the years he had become an extension of myself. Without Martin I could not have coped with nursing my mother at home. He had acted like a counterweight, a balance. We had managed a sort of routine, in a situation that verged on the impossible, of bucking each other up. Holding on against the odds, what the doctors had said to me, that we would last two weeks, if that. But we had endured much longer and would, I think, have gone the distance if Martin had been younger. Had *he* been at home, I would not have been with Paula in the hotel. Neither would I have been in jail or had a stay of days in hospital. As it was I could never forget his passing. Some nights I started awake and thought it a dream, a bad one, until I looked at his couch and he was not there. The house was forlorn then. I was forlorn and all unsure, and it would not have been the first time that I had telephoned my sister in the middle of the night.

I had been far from a man in the first few weeks when Martin was no more. At a loose end? I had been an angry man, but there are many angry men in Glasgow. I can vouch for that. And it is no joke, not when you are older, to be battered up and down the street. When you sober up you feel a clown and thank the Lord you have not been maimed. That aside, you are set on edge for some time after, until you chance to take a drink again and logic goes out of the window. It had happened before and could happen again and I dreaded to think how it could end. It is so easy to forget, to take a drink. To protect myself, I went round to the chapel house and took a three-month pledge to abstain from alcohol. Father Reilly was understanding and said that he would pray for me, that I would recover from the loss of Martin and my addiction to strong drink. He invoked a lot of saints, even John the Baptist. I thanked the priest, and leaving him I felt a new calm, less on edge. But I was still missing Martin.

I would go on missing Martin for a long, long time. Father Reilly was not in the best of health himself, when he administered my pledge. I know now, if I did not know it then, that he had cancer and had not long to live. But he still had time to talk and calm me down. He was a good and pious man. I often say a prayer for him.

I had put it to Paula point-blank: could I go home with her?

'No strings?' she said.

'No strings,' I said. 'I'm only lonely.'

'I was lonely too,' she said. 'I wanted you as much as you wanted me.'

'You don't know how much I wanted you.'

'I have some idea, an old thing like me.'

'I like being with you.'

'You needed someone, didn't you?'

'I told you I was lonely.'

I made love with Paula in a tender, almost healing way. Sex can heal? I felt it could, in bed with her. For that little while before we slept.

I felt down the length of her nose with a finger.

'Do you like long noses?'

'I think I must. I was once in love with a Jewish girl. I wanted to run away with her, to go to London, but she stood me up at the railway station.'

'That must have been a long time ago, if you wanted to *run* away.'

'It was the autumn of 1961. I was seventeen. Sarah was

one year younger. I have always regretted that she did not come, that we did not go together to London.'

'Did you see her again, after she stood you up?'

'I did. I met her a few years later, but it was not the same. She had changed and so had I. Our time was *then*, but Sarah did not know it.'

'She was young.'

'So was I.'

'Did you not find another lover?'

'I might have done, but I did not find another her. There was no other girl I would have gone to London with.'

That night, in Paula's bed, was my first sound sleep since Martin. We had spoken into the small hours, and she was not a psychiatrist for nothing. I'd opened up to her about my being drunk and the hospital and how, just days before, I had taken a three-month pledge.

'It's about all I've got to hang on to.'

'Have you always been religious?'

'No, and I'm not religious now, not really. I don't even go to mass on Sundays.'

'Then why did you go to see the priest?'

'He was my last hope.'

I was surprised at just how well Paula had retained her body. In truth, she had quite a body for any age: all trim and neat.

'I had no other place to go to.'

'You could have gone to Alcoholics Anonymous.'

'I have already been to Alcoholics Anonymous.'

'It didn't help?'

'It couldn't have, I continued to drink.'

'But Martin stopped you drinking?'

'He *contained* my drinking. I wanted to keep him and I could not have kept him if I had continued to drink the way I had.'

'If you contained it then, can't you contain it now, without Martin?'

'I think that I might prefer to stop it altogether.'

'That would be the wisest thing to do.' Paula cuddled in on me. 'Sleep tight, my love.'

In the morning Paula drove me home.

'Will I see you tonight?' I asked.

'No, not tonight. I have arranged to go some place tonight.'

'Tomorrow night, then?'

'You are insistent, aren't you?'

'I want to see you again.'

'I'm too old for you.'

'We agreed no strings.'

'I'm still too old for you.'

'This is silly.'

'It would be sillier still to become involved.'

'You don't need to become involved.'

'I'm a *woman*, Thomas.' It was still dark and there was a drizzling rain. Paula had her eyes on the road. 'In a couple of weeks I'd *be* involved, whether I wanted to be or not.'

I saw her again, in the hospital, but it was never on for another night together. With regard to my books, we both forgot them. I could never forget her, though. Our one-night stand had been worth a year of loving. How I had felt! I was none too sure if I could keep my three-month pledge. I was hanging on, taking one day at a time. It is all we have, when you come down to it. I had hoped to have a thing with Paula, companionship and sex. I would have preferred Martin, without the sex; so perhaps she had been right in chucking me. Before I chucked her? For, for all I liked to be with her, I would have begun to fancy younger women, and Paula, who was no fool, had known that.

I stayed inside over Christmas and New Year 1993–4. I'd be fifty in February. Half a century. Hitler had been alive when I was born and many a man had yet to fall before the war was over. I had an uncle who fell at Anzio, after I was born. Looking at it that way, fifty years is a long time. But I could remember back to when I was one or two, and from that perspective it did not seem so very long. It sometimes seemed like yesterday that I was a boy and reading *Billy Bunter*. My mother had been born in 1910. I have photos of her when she was a child, in bare feet, on the street, sometime during the First World War. She had been coming then, as she was going now: her short visit on this earth.

I had thought to visit the chapel at Christmas time, but had been too depressed to make the effort. A hospital nurse had suggested that I go to AA, for some company if nothing else. It had not been a bad suggestion, but I could not be bothered with that place either. I watched late-night movies on television. On Hogmanay I watched a New Year's party, *Auld Lang Syne*. I did not take a cup to toast, but I was severely tempted. I had a bottle of whisky in the house and such was the extent of my temptation that I poured it down the sink. You do not get bottles of whisky for nothing, and I had been saving that one until my pledge was up. I was counting the days till then, when I would feel free to drink again. After a most trembling start, my nerves had began to knit together and I was able to sleep again at nights.

This was well into January. Such is the damage of alcohol on the nervous system. It is a very lucky alcoholic who survives to go to the fellowship in anything like one piece.

My mother's health was worsening by the day, if not the hour. There was nothing of her now, in body bulk. Her skin was thin and loose and it had a scaly look. But she was always glad to see me and, as weak as she was, would reach out with her one good arm. When I spoke to her she would grin and nod. She looked not unlike ET, the 'extraterrestrial' in the film of that name. I told my mother that I had taken the pledge and that Martin was fit and well. The nights outside were lightening but, inside that hospital, I knew she would not live to see the summer. It was something of a miracle that she had survived this long, but she could not survive much longer. She could not have weighed four stone, if that. Her voice was gone and she had no memory, but for some reason, she was still there—reaching out to me.

I did not drink when my pledge was completed in February or early March. Paula's father had died early in the New Year and I had missed her in the hospital. I had had no woman since, nor had I tried to get a woman. The inclination was not there, faced as I was with death.

In mid-April my mother lapsed into a coma because of a chest infection. I did not need a doctor to tell me that there was little if any chance of her recovering this time. I already knew it in my bones when I saw she was unconscious. They moved her out of the ward into a private room. I would sit at the side of the bed and touch her hand. I hoped that she would depart like that, just sleep away.

She died the following month, in May of 1994. I received a telephone call from the hospital telling me that she had passed away. It was a Saturday morning. I sat in my chair and looked to where her special chair used to be. It all now seemed like another life when I had her and Martin.

I thanked whoever it was who had telephoned. Death, however expected, is always sudden, and my mother's was no exception. I had seen her only hours before and had known that the end was near, but it was still a shock that she was dead. A tingle in my spine. I could barely believe that she was no more. I was alone in the house and I wished that I had Martin. We would have gone out for a walk, I think. Had my mother *known* that he was dead when I said he was okay? She could usually tell when I was lying. It was one to ponder, even if I would never know. There are some things sometimes it is better not to know. She had been moved to the hospital mortuary. I would need to arrange for undertakers to take her body out of there and bury her beside my father, who had died so long ago.

My sister phoned and we spoke for a while, consoling one another. Our mother had been eighty-four and one month old when she had passed away, or *over*.

Later, alone in the empty house, I tried to pull myself together, out of a huge despondency. I was more alone than I have ever been, and then: '*Oh, hello, John.*' My mother's voice was vibrant, full of joy. She sounded as though, wherever she was, in whatever void, she had had a wonderful surprise. Those three words were all she spoke, in a voice I had thought to have forgotten, that I had last heard when I was a toddler. It was the voice of my mother in her prime, much younger than I was now. It was as odd, this reversal in our ages, as hearing my mother speak. Until then I had not believed in a spirit world. But here, some four hours after her death, she was in a new adventure, could you call it that, beyond the human ken.

After those three words there was only silence. I looked to where her chair had been, and felt better that she had escaped from it, a life of pain and suffering. But at the same time I was slightly miffed that she was not at all concerned as to how *we* were, my sister and I. Her son and daughter. It was now all *John,* who had been her husband, our father. He had waited a damn long time for her, had John. Anyhow, it was nice to know that, in some way, they had been reunited.

Years later I acquired a girlfriend who was into spiritualism. We went together for a couple of months and though it did not interest me at all, I went to a spiritualist meeting with her. The medium was a thin fierce-looking woman from Ulster. I had never seen her in my life. My girlfriend had told me she was good—which, as things turned out, was quite an understatement.

We sang a couple of hymns (in proper pews, for it was a church) before matters got under way. We were about thirty souls, mostly women—I think there were only two other men—in the group. The medium stood at the front, facing us, and almost immediately she had a *message*. 'I have a man with me who breaks stones with a big, big hammer.' She paused for a moment's concentration. 'I can *hear* him break the stones.'

Of course, my father had been a quarryman, breaking stones for many years, and I had no doubt that it was him connecting with the medium. But I said nothing. Soon she became frustrated and looked round the people in the church. Someone should raise their hand! When no one did she almost stamped her feet in temper. 'I have him with me.'

I had gone to the church to please my girlfriend, nothing else. I most certainly did not want a message. I had not even thought that you could receive a message. Spiritualism had been mumbo-jumbo business to me. But it should not have been, for I already knew that dying was not the end. Far from it. But I did not want to become involved with what I could not understand and I am sure that my father, that saintly man, has long forgiven me.

My mother was buried beside my father in St Peter's Cemetery in Glasgow's East End. It is not far from Celtic Park, where Billy Graham had spoken. Father Reilly said the mass and came out to the grave-side with me.

My sister had been in the chapel, but she could not face St Peter's. I had not told her of my experience, for there is a saying in the Catholic Church that you should leave the dead in peace, which, I think, is very true, that the living should not consult the dead. *Requiescant in pace.*

Father Reilly had aged into an old man since the last time I had seen him. In fact it had demanded all of his effort to make it from the car to the grave, to say the prayers after they had lowered down the coffin in a sun-drenched graveyard. I remembered Father Reilly out with his dog, and me with Martin. I had thought him for a rather fragile, pale-faced man. A gentle person. Which he was. Both him and his dog, his Labrador. I had not thought—who would?—that our relationship would end like this, my mother in her coffin and Father Reilly, his face a bright copper colour, halfway in a box himself.

It came as no surprise when I heard that he had passed over two or three weeks later.

I was drinking again. On and off, trying to control it— what cannot be controlled. I had suffered thirty years in self-denial, that I could take a drink or leave it. What madness, for I knew in my heart that *one* drink was enough to do for me. But I persisted, as only an alcoholic would. Finally, I found myself in a hospital in Las Palmas, in Tenerife.

It was about the fourth week of my current drinking bout. It had got out of hand—if it ever was in hand, that is, for I had been house-drinking in the mornings within days of my mother's death. Suffice to say that I was not sober when I booked a two-week holiday in Tenerife. It was a late-night departure, and I drank the best part of a litre bottle of Jack Daniel's whisky in the airport toilet.

I remember little of the flight or of Tenerife. How I got into the hospital I do not know. The chances are that I had been in a fight, for my ribs were cracked and my eye was cut and one side of my face was bruised and hugely swollen. Was this the start of something new, my awakening in hospitals? I would have preferred a police cell. At least there you knew that you were *whole,* unlike in a hospital. I could have lost a leg for all I knew, or both legs. It is a scary thing to awake in a hospital bed and not know why you are in that bed. It was a total blackout. The last I could remember I was drinking the whisky in the toilet outside the departure gate at Glasgow Airport.

I was detained in hospital for six days. They ran a battery of tests. Why not? I was insured and everything was itemized. A Dr Diaz was in charge, and so that the insurance would pay the hospital, I had told him that I had been mugged. Which I might have been, for all I knew. For all that Diaz knew either, and it suited him to go along with the mugging story. The police were called to the hospital and while I was on a drip for dehydration, I repeated my story to them. I was supposed to be on holiday. My only views of the island were from a hospital window. At the end of the six days I was ambulanced out to the airport and wheelchaired on to an aeroplane and the next I knew, for I was heavily sedated—Diaz had been taking no chances, given my sudden withdrawal from alcohol—I was back in Glasgow.

As soon as I was home I drained a glass of whisky. After what had happened and where I'd been, I felt entitled to the whisky. I can remember the feeling when it hit my gut and the heat spread out. It banished all my worries. I thought to get some money back, to show a profit, by claiming on the insurance. But at the back of my head I must have known that something had to give, that I could not go on this way. I did not want this zombie walk, in and out of hospitals, to go on for too much longer.

Late that summer, for something to do, I began to attend the Tuesday night novena to St Anthony in the Gorbals. It was not the same without Martin; and when I said so to my sister she agreed to come to the novena with me. I had the idea of trying to attend the nine consecutive Tuesdays. I was still sceptical, to say the least, about religion. That did not stop me praying, though, and I prayed for peace of mind.

Mary had moved into a house not far from me and we would meet up and walk down to the Gorbals together. We would sometimes try, in this new place, to figure out where our old street had been so long ago. It did not seem so long ago, standing at the gas-lit corners, fooling with the girls. We both agreed that where the old street had been there was now a row of terraced houses. But enough of memories, for I was striving for a future. I wanted to write again, to try my best and hope for luck. But I had written nothing for nearly three years, and that is a long time for a writer not to write, if he *is* a writer. I was full of doubt if I was one.

This nag to write did not come on suddenly. More a gradual thing that I had tried to cast aside. I had certainly put it off. A dread to fight with words again? It would be fair to say I was twice frightened: of alcohol and words.

★ * ★

On the eighth Tuesday Mary asked if I had ever heard of the Pioneer movement of total abstinence. I told her that I had and that Father Reilly had been a member.

'He used to drink, did you know that?'

'No, I didn't. I thought that he was just teetotal.'

'After he became a Pioneer he was teetotal.'

'I wouldn't have thought that Father Reilly ever drank.'

'Neither would I, but he told me he did, when he was a young priest.'

Mary said that the Pioneers were meeting that coming Sunday. 'At three o'clock, in St Columbkille's in Rutherglen.'

'How did you find that out?'

'Someone told me in the chapel.'

Rutherglen is a small town on the edge of Glasgow, only a walk away from where I stayed.

'It would do no harm if you went.'

'Would you come with me if I went?'

She agreed and I told her I would go, but by midday Wednesday I was drinking. Mary was very, very disappointed. When I began to drink it usually went on for days, until I was either ill or injured. I don't know why I began to drink. That was no surprise, for I never did. You might just say I took the notion. It is as simple a way of explaining it as I can manage. I had walked out in the morning, direct to the nearest pub. There was no sway, no should I or should I not. I wanted a drink, and I would *have* a drink. That is the hard fact of it. What it had always been, regardless of the consequences. I had one Tuesday of the nine to go to complete the full novena. I had not given a thought to it when I had lifted the first drink. A pint of beer, for what it matters. As the day wore on I became very drunk and I don't remember much of it. I awoke the following morning in my chair, still fully dressed. When I made to rise, to go to the toilet—for a pee in the sink, if I am honest—I tripped over a bag of booze. Cans of beer and a full bottle of whisky. I felt badly in need of a drink of it, the whisky. After my pee I poured a glass and diluted it with water. For some reason I thought to say the rosary, that I did not end up in hospital. This was my first drink for quite some while and it would be lousy luck, or so I thought, if I ended up in hospital. I did not think of the city morgue; why, I do not know. For I *should* have thought of that grim place, drinking whisky in the morning—or, given a bit more accuracy, in the middle of the night.

What happened over the next two days I do not know. I could have been on the moon for all I knew. Or in a disused brickworks. I neglected to wash or shave or brush my teeth or anything civilized. On the morning of the fourth day, which was a Saturday, I must have glimpsed some sanity and I held back from the bottle all that day. For some strange reason it was not too hard, and I wanted to get sober. Why? I had money enough to continue drinking, and it was a new feeling this, in the middle of a drinking bout, that I wanted to become sober.

I discovered that I had lost a tooth, a front crown. It was no big deal. Better that than I had lost an eye. There are plenty of one-eyed guys walking about as a direct result of the drinking game. My front tooth was nothing.

I choose to think that it is the power of prayer, of the good people who had prayed for me, that took me to the Pioneer meeting the following day, the Sunday. *And* my sister. It was her suggestion, after all. We went together, with a friend, and after we had learned what it entailed to be a Pioneer—you say a short prayer twice a day and wear an emblem of the Sacred Heart, a pin as the Pioneers call it—we, all three, volunteered for membership.

The Pioneer movement was founded by a Dublin priest, Father Cullen, in 1899. Father Cullen's original idea was for a small, women-only movement that would afford a good example in a troubled, drunken Ireland. It was not meant for problem drinkers, for guys like me. Most Pioneers have never drunk or, if they have, drunk sparingly. You can go to a Pioneer meeting and, outwith the prayer at the beginning and end, forget the purpose of your visit, for alcohol is seldom mentioned. The active membership is small, about thirty people in the whole of Glasgow. We meet on the first Sunday of each month and sometimes go to special night-time masses. This is when a new member will receive their pin. The event will be recorded in the Pioneer headquarters in Dublin. For full membership you must be an adult who believes in Christ and the Sacred Heart and be drink-free for at least one year.

Both Mary and our friend became full members on the day, but I had to make do with a temporary membership. I would receive a small red emblem rather than a full, white one. I didn't care and I wore that emblem proudly for two years. I think I knew I would not drink but hesitated in departing with my *right* to drink, the solemn vow of the Pioneer. You can be stubborn about the most silly things, or I could. I can still be. The Pioneers were offering a life of sobriety and, for the first time since Martin had died, I felt that I could live it. Yet still I balked. Some rebellious streak, that I kept my options open. What folly! I had no option. Another drink could well have been the death of me, but I dithered. My sister asked me what was wrong and I told her I did not know.

'Don't you think that you can do it?'

★ * ★

I had been a Pioneer for more than a year when I went to stay at Pluscarden Abbey, a Benedictine monastery in the north of Scotland. I spent ten days with the monks. It is a place of peace and holiness and a true refuge for a man like me. I had lost my way, or perhaps had never found it. All my life I had wanted to be a part of something, but I had allowed myself to be a part of nothing. Not a thing. My sister recommended Pluscarden Abbey to me, where I took a vow of silence because I did not wish to speak to my fellow guests.

Pluscarden Abbey is some six miles outside of Elgin in Morayshire, and on a cold clear day in the middle of December, I alighted from the train and walked up to the abbey. My room consisted of a small table, a chair and a narrow bed. The window looked over fields into woods where, I would discover, there was a shack which housed a hermit. I believe that the monks provided his food and water. Closeted monks and a hidden hermit: it was a strange, new world to me.

I had arrived at Pluscarden in the early afternoon, still speaking. My vow of silence had not been premeditated. Inside the abbey, I happened to hear that certain monks had taken a vow of silence. Given the mood that I was in, it seemed like a good way out for me too.

The abbot was a tall, well-mannered man who shook my hand. When I mentioned my intention, he asked if I had taken such a vow before. I told him that I had not.

'It is not the easiest thing to do.'

'I want to do it.'

'Why do you want to do it?'

'I don't feel like speaking.'

'I thought you might have said to feel closer to God.'

'No, I just don't want to speak.'

The abbot had a paper with my name and address and some details about me.

'You will be with us for ten days, is that correct?'

I told him that it was and that I intended to maintain my vow until I left the abbey.

'When do you intend to begin this vow?'

'As soon as I leave you.'

It is a strange thing, a vow of silence. The abbot had passed the word about among the monks and my fellow guests—there were usually about five of them—and it was accepted as a normal thing, more or less, that I could not speak. Keeping silent did not bother me, not until I met a monk whom I used to know. He had been a barman in a public house in Victoria Road in Glasgow, a pretty rowdy place. He had served me drink a few times there. His name was Brother Finbar. We smiled one to the other, and he put a finger to his mouth.

I was to see him a whole lot more in the monastery. In his brown cassock and bare sandalled feet, eating with a spoon. All of the monks ate with a spoon out of a bowl. The spoon and the bowl and the clothes they wore were all they owned.

As soon as I saw Finbar I regretted my vow. But I was stuck with it, and I did not want to cheat. Still, it was good to see a familiar face, and Finbar seemed to have found his niche in life. This—as years before, when a new priest had been ordained—had me wondering about where I was and what was wrong that I had as been forced to come to this place.

My first morning began at nine o'clock, when I had breakfast. It was self-service and I ate porridge and drank a couple of cups of coffee. I then went to ten o'clock mass. The chapel was high and narrow with stained-glass windows, and there were women there, at the service. They had come up from St Cecilia's—St Cecilia was a sister of St Benedict, who had founded the Benedictines—which was a women-only guest house at the outskirts of the abbey. On my first visit to the chapel I almost spoke to one of them, to bid the time of day, but I caught myself in the nick of time with a palms out, helpless gesture. The woman had a look of astonishment on her face. How to explain? I could not ask for a pen and paper, so had to walk away. The next time that I saw her I think she knew about my vow, for if she did not speak she was not unpleasant either.

I began to go on long walks, some as many as ten miles, and on those lonely hikes I thought about Martin quite a bit. How *he* would have loved to have been here, in the open countryside. Then again, had he been around we would have been nowhere near a monastery. I would have shunned the thought if Martin had still been with me, or had I still been drinking or had a girlfriend. But I had no one I could relate to, except my sister, and there are some things that you cannot tell a sister. There had been a lot in my life that my sister did not know about, and I hoped she never would.

I had completed three days of silence before I began to pray. A few Our Fathers. I was walking when I said them, remembered words from my early childhood. In the Glasgow of the 1950s you were taught to pray at a very young age, about five or six, if you went to a Catholic school. This was called religious education and you were told about your guardian angel. Whoever had been assigned to me had had his work cut out. The luck of the draw, for I could not see any angel asking for such a man. The Our Fathers did no harm and I returned to the monastery in better spirit than when I had set out.

There were two evening services, Compline and Vespers, and I was a regular at both. All through the day, I would look forward to the evening, for Compline and Vespers in the dimly lit chapel. It was quiet and soothing. The chanting monks came out on to the altar two by two. The praying was in Latin. This, in the monastery, was the first for a long time that I had heard Latin in a chapel. It suited the place and the hooded monks. We were as insulated, detached from the world and suspended in time.

Soon after Vespers, about eight o'clock, the lights went out inside the abbey. This time was called the Great Silence. Nobody was supposed to speak, and I would sit up reading in my room. There was a feeling of goodness about the place and it was the first for a long time that I felt at peace, at home. Of course, it was not my home, and I would soon need to leave Pluscarden. Modern monasteries do not encourage guests to stay for much longer than ten days. On a close look I would think that correct and right, as, given much longer, you could find it hard to readjust to the world outside.

I found it easy, the not speaking. Towards the end of my

stay in Pluscarden, I tried to be up at four o'clock for the first mass of the day. A short one of fifteen or twenty minutes. It was enough, in a freezing chapel. I would look out for Finbar among the monks, and if I could not understand why he had become a monk, I had seldom seen a man so happy, so content with his lot. I would hurry back from the four o'clock mass to the comfort of my room and my bed, where I could only marvel at Finbar and his fellow monks and their true love of God.

It was a much truer love than I had. My mistake in those last days was to treat religion as a punishment—what four o'clock morning masses were to me. Rather than help they had served to hinder, to give me doubts as to why I was in such a place at such an hour and under a vow of silence. I was confused about the whole thing. I have come to believe that religion should be joyful, as *tambourine* as you can make it in this day and age. The monks are in a world apart, and what is right for them—like the four o'clock morning masses—can be wrong and harmful for someone else. Someone like me. On my last day I was still in bed at four o'clock and I wondered what I had been about, attending these early masses.

Snow fell when I waited for Finbar outside the chapel on my last day in the monastery. A Christmas feel, even if it was long past Christmas. I had my bag packed and I was ready to go, to walk to Elgin and board the train back again to Glasgow. Ten days. It felt, waiting for Finbar, that I had come here yesterday. But a nostalgic feeling for all of that, and I think I knew that I would return to this never-changing world. The place suited me. I could be myself, whatever that was, and, most important of all, I had learned to pray again.

The cassocked Finbar put out his hand, a smile. 'You are leaving us, I hear,' he said.

I tried to say that I was indeed, but the words came out all choked and croaked and, I thought, barely comprehensible.

Finbar laughed. 'It will take a day or two to find your voice again.'

I was in no hurry to find my voice, but outside the chapel in the snow, I would have liked to have spoken to Finbar.

'Another time,' he said.

Standing in the falling snow, so white and pure, my last day in the monastery. *He who is without sin.* I had been to confession and Holy Communion and, by the laws of the Catholic Church, had been cleansed of all my sins. It was a wonderful feeling, though I knew it would not last and I would soon be stained with sin again. I needed a woman to touch and hold, to make love to.

'I shall come back,' I said.

'I know you will.'

And that was it. Lacking a voice in the snow in Pluscarden, there was no way that I could have had a meaningful conversation. Still, Finbar gave me a set of rosary beads, my first rosary beads since I had been a child at my First Communion. I have prized them to this day.

On my arrival back in Glasgow I was shocked by the noise and the mass of people. If my room at the monastery had been available, waiting for me, I would have returned there and taken another vow of silence.

There was a lot to wonder, to think about, in regard to my stay in the abbey. What had I gained, if anything? An uplift of the spirit? I did *feel* better, but there had been no spiritual awakening. I was very much the same person with the same doubts about myself and about religion as when I had first gone to Pluscarden. Ten days are not enough to change a man, his basic being. But much as I relished the silence, I knew I needed people. This was a first acceptance that I was a prideful man and that pride had stopped my taking the pledge for the remainder of my days. I had preferred to think that I could do it alone, without the Pioneers and the Pioneer prayer that had kept me sober so far. That sort of pride you can do without, and all my years I had been full of it. Some weird attempt to prove I was a man when I had been nothing more than a drunken clown. It was time, and more than time, that I accepted this flaw in my nature—the sin of pride, for it was nothing less—and I determined, with the help of God, to try and overcome it.

It took a few days for my voice to return to normal after I left Pluscarden. Mary considered my recovery in the Pioneers as little short of a miracle, and so did I for that matter. I had no urge or need to drink. I said my prayer twice a day. On the literary front I had been commissioned to write a boxing memoir, about what boxing had meant to me. This was a joy of a book to write and I was well paid for writing it. I had been on holiday to France and Spain. I was a sober man, and this was a whole new experience. Another country, another me. Some people asked what my pin signified, and I told them that I was a Pioneer and then had to explain what being a Pioneer meant. But did I know? I had yet to make a full commitment, and, in theory, I could drink at any time. This state of affairs could not go on. I was walking on thin ice. In November of 1997, I vowed to God never to drink again.

Looking back down the years, I have to accept that Martin was a gift from God, to keep me in the world. Why, I do not know. I did not have a faith in God in 1983, but through changing times and different kinds of me, I think I have it now. Billy Graham made a huge impression at a time when I was struggling, when everything I knew said no, that there was no God. And it suited me to think that way, given the life I had led. But, in a halting, almost grudging way, I was drawn to religion. The novenas I had made with Martin. Father Reilly. The first Midnight Masses with my mother. There is so much I do not know, but I am sure there is a living God and that I shall meet with Martin once again, one day somewhere. That is my belief.

ACKNOWLEDGMENTS

★ ＊ ★

Rosaleen Pollock typed out my manuscript and encouraged me at times when I was struggling. The original idea for this book came from Rosie Boycott when she was the editor at *Esquire*. Thanks to the staff at Granta, where Ian Jack and Helen Gordon took an early interest in this work. My editor, Matt Weiland, deserves a special thanks for work above and beyond the usual.